Empowering the Oppressed

Empowering the Oppressed

Grassroots Advocacy Movements in India

John G. Sommer

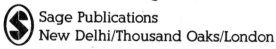

Sage Publications
New Delhi/Thousand Oaks/London

First published in 2001 by

Sage Publications India Pvt Ltd
M 32 Market, Greater Kailash I
New Delhi 110 048

Sage Publications Inc
2455 Teller Road
Thousand Oaks, California 91320

Sage Publications Ltd
6 Bonhill Street
London EC2A 4PU

Published by Tejeshwar Singh for Sage Publications India Pvt Ltd, typeset by Asian Telelinks in Palatino 10pt. and printed at Chaman Enterprises, New Delhi.

Third Printing 2002

Library of Congress Cataloging-in-Publication Data

Sommer, John, 1941–
 Empowering the oppressed: grassroots advocacy movements in India/John G. Sommer.
  p. cm.
 Includes bibliographical references.
  1. Poor—Services for—India. 2. Dalits—Services for—India. 3. Poor—Civil rights—India. 4. Dalits—Civil rights—India. 5. Social advocacy—India. 6. Political activists—India. I. Title.

ISBN: 0–7619–9572–2 (US–HB)
   0–7619–9573–0 (US–PB)

81–7829–060–X (India–HB)
81–7829–061–8 (India–PB)

Sage Production Team: Dipika Nath, M.S.V. Namboodiri, and Santosh Rawat

Contents

Foreword

Empowering the Oppressed is the wrong title for this book. A reading of its contents suggests that it could more appropriately be titled Disempowering the Oppressor. When the poor 'extricate them-selves from a system of bondage', they are more than creating a space for their own improvement. They are changing the 'system' itself at its core. Again when the union of workers organized by SEWA is able to enforce minimum wages which law enforcing agencies fail to enforce or the employers stoutly resist, the character of the system as a whole undergoes transformation. This is the stuff that is served here to the readers, thanks to all the participants in the making of this book and to John Sommer, who detected the common idiom and ethos in seemingly diverse situations: off with the oppressors.

We have a feast here of real life experiences of numerous organizations and individuals across India relating to the struggle of the oppressed. Sharing will multiply the value of these experi-ences. They provide filtered fuel for those similarly engaged in other parts of India—and perhaps also for those in other countries with comparable conditions.

The circumference of this printed matter is larger than what is bound in its nine chapters. To taste its full impact, reading in one sitting is highly recommended. I say it from my own fruitful jour-ney through the manuscript of this book.

—L.C. Jain

Preface

After more than 30 years of working with international development organizations around the globe, I considered myself reasonably well informed about the range of activities being undertaken
to improve the livelihoods of the world's poor. A number of these
activities were inspiring, effective, and contributing importantly
to improving the human condition. Many of the individuals carrying them out—in Africa, Asia and Latin America—were, and are,
impressive in their altruism, commitment and professionalism.
They include workers from a host of international organizations,
government and non-government (NGOs), and from an ever-
burgeoning number of local voluntary groups.

During the early 1970s, for example, when I was living in India
and working for The Ford Foundation, I once had occasion to spend
a couple of days visiting an unusually impressive rural boarding
school led by a widely known and respected Gandhian gentleman.
It was located in a particularly downtrodden part of the country,
where the population was described as 'sub-human'—a term not
intended to be derogatory but rather, an honest admission of the
primitive conditions endured by the people; conditions reflected
in the very dullness in their eyes, indeed in their entire expression
and being. The children in this school were learning reading, writ-
ing and the basics of sanitation and garden agriculture, and it was
thought that by removing them from their desperate home settings
and boarding them in this more progressive school environment,
more modern attitudes would take root. It was believed that these,

in turn, would result in their ability to subsequently improve their own and their families' living conditions in the surrounding villages. In such a downtrodden and relatively remote setting, the prospects seemed difficult, but hopeful. Almost 30 years later, by happy circumstance, I came to meet this Gandhian leader again; by now he had been working there for 46 years. I asked him what progress he had been able to observe in that time. Shockingly, his answer was 'None', though he added that perhaps the households and surrounding gardens were a little neater. He said that the state of the society was so deeply entrenched that it may take four or five generations before any significant improvement could be seen.

In the mid 1970s, I had been asked by the Overseas Development Council to conduct what, surprisingly, turned out to be the first broad-ranging analysis of the changing role of US private and voluntary organizations in third world development. The resulting book was titled *Beyond Charity*, and it was a reflection of the shift then beginning from predominantly relief and social welfare activities to more self-sustaining development projects. The catch phrase of the time was that to ensure lasting success, one had to 'teach the man to fish, not to give fish handouts'. Yet in those days, it was not widely recognized, or acknowledged, that structural and political obstacles often impeded even the best fisherman's ability to achieve a satisfactory standard of living. That, furthermore, these factors often left him (not to mention her) deprived of guarantees of human rights and social justice. It was also clear that by focusing primarily on discrete *projects* rather than on the more integrated *processes* of development, accomplishments on one plane could easily be diminished or negated on another. Otherwise (admittedly at the risk of over-simplification), how could one explain the persistence—indeed, often worsening—of poverty and injustice amongst the world's poor after decades of assistance and billions of dollars of expenditure? How else could one explain the lack of significant change generated by that boarding school in India?

In 1994, I was invited to join the newly created advisory board of the Unitarian-Universalist Association's Holdeen India Program (HIP). As I came to know some of the leaders of their partner groups, and subsequently visited with them and observed their work in India, I quickly realized that they were following the most sophisticated and effective approaches I had yet seen. Having continued, after my period of Ford Foundation residence, to regularly visit India as dean of the School for International Training, I was not unfamiliar with either the subcontinent and its problems or with the many inspiring development efforts being undertaken on many levels throughout the country. But there was definitely something special, in my experience, about these groups, most of which had begun working only during the previous decade. Realizing how relatively unknown they are, in India as well as abroad, I thus felt it important to let others concerned with human development and social justice know of their experiences.

In preparing this book, the respective efforts of several of the Indian groups and of the Holdeen India Program to assess their work and compile and compare lessons learned, provided valuable information and insights. This was multiplied during intensive meetings held in early 2000 among some 30 leaders whose organizations are listed in Annexure 2. The sharing that took place during these meetings, on a rural campus in Thane district, Maharashtra, with previous sessions having been held in Ahmedabad, Gujarat, generated much of the wisdom recounted in these pages, particularly in Chapter Seven.

As usual, acknowledgements of inspiration and help provided to an author tend to be inadequate to their importance to the resultant publication. Certainly that would be the case with respect to the leaders whose work forms the subject of this book. While some may find the tone of the descriptions overly glorified, with insufficient attention to the inevitable 'warts' in their efforts, I can only respond by saying that, truth to tell, and as corroborated by more than one outside observer, the latter are truly hard to find. I owe them much gratitude, both for their inspiration and for their assistance in helping me and others understand the facts and lessons of their experience.

Along with these Indian leaders, I must single out Kathy Sreedhar, HIP's director since its inception in 1984. She too has been an inspiration, and more than anyone else, has given of her time, commitment, intelligence and enthusiasm to help me track down and make sense of a huge and complex amount of information and experience. Also critical to the undertaking has been John Buehrens, president of the Unitarian-Universalist Association until mid-2001; he has been a bulwark of support, both moral and practical, ensuring optimal resources not only for this lessons learned initiative, but for the work of the Holdeen India Program as a whole. My colleagues on the HIP advisory board and a number of other professional colleagues and friends who have reviewed and offered helpful suggestions on various portions of the manuscript also have my sincere appreciation and thanks.

Dummerston, Vermont, USA
March 2001

Introduction

The solution to poverty is generally understood to be 'development'—a cause embraced by governments, multilateral institutions and thousands of non-government, voluntary organizations around the world. In the name of development, they have substantially contributed in recent decades to improved agricultural production, sanitation, health care, schooling and income levels of the poor. Yet the poor—not to mention those labelled as the poorest of the poor, who have always been hard to reach—are still with us. Indeed, the evidence suggests that in the current era of fast-paced technological change and galloping globalization, the gap between the rich and the poor is widening. Without denying positive accomplishments to date, it is clear that today's typical approaches to development, and to donor assistance in support thereof, are desperately insufficient to the problem at hand.

This book introduces some unique groups in India that have found strikingly effective ways to improve the lot of the poorest of the poor. The leaders whose stories are told here are committed to the empowerment of their most oppressed fellow countrymen and women to organize and press for their full citizen rights. Where the traditional development approach has focused on 'teaching the man to fish' as distinct from the relief approach of giving a fish handout, these leaders are going a step further. To them, it is clear that without free access to waters containing fish, and the absence of resources to obtain fishing nets and effectively market the fish caught, knowledge of fishing is not enough. The groups described here have learned from experience that without the power to access resources, without equal opportunity, the poor do not have the necessary sustainable foundation on which to 'develop'. Development projects, therefore, will not solve the basic problems of poverty. In contrast to most groups dedicated to improving the human condition, these groups have decided to focus on realigning power relationships so that poor people can pursue their own just demands of government and of society at large.

There are, of course, many approaches to realigning power relationships. In India alone, Gandhian and Marxist groups have been most active, the one following a strictly non-violent approach and the other, through the Naxalite movement, including violence as a way to pursue its aims. In addition, India has produced a number of communal, ethnic, gender and other identity movements, not to mention a broad range of issue-based movements, such as those opposing large dam projects that threaten displacement and cause hardship for significant numbers of (usually poor) Indians.

The leaders of some of the groups described in this book have themselves come out of the Gandhian and, in at least one case, Naxalite movements. All are content to, indeed insist upon, working within the context and framework of the Indian constitution and state structures. They seek greater impact than today's Gandhian institutions seem able to achieve by relying on social welfare as opposed to pursuing political empowerment activities. Or perhaps they should be seen as today's *mahatmas*, minus the atrophy that too often seeps into movements after the founder's departure from the scene. Gandhiji's own task during the pre-Independence period in India was arguably easier than today's challenges. Although he opposed all forms of oppression and talked of 'structural violence' as well as blatant physical violence, the primary focus of his historic struggle was against a highly visible colonial power. Modern India's sources of oppression—the 'new colonialism', in the form of social hierarchies—are less immediately visible to the eye; they are more diffuse, more thoroughly entrenched in the culture, and certainly unsusceptible to being packed onto ships and planes and removed from the country.

The leaders of the groups introduced here, along with those of about two dozen other grassroots empowerment movements, have begun to compare experiences and lessons learned from their recent years' struggles for human rights and social justice. While no account could fully convey the richness of their discussions, the current volume attempts to suggest, as much as possible, the flavour of some of their experiences, in their own words, as written in their documents and orally conveyed in meetings together. More importantly, it conveys their analysis of the major lessons learned, with a view to assisting the efforts of others concerned with promoting meaningful and durable improvements in the lives of the poor. Although there is much that is unique in their Indian context, the broader approaches discussed should be applicable in most countries—and not only in what is commonly known as the 'developing world'.

This book is also about outside assistance and its role in the empowerment approach to development. Frequently, discussions of development and aid become completely intertwined—not surprisingly perhaps, since donors often exert strong influence over the activities they fund. Indeed, some argue that foreign aid, in particular, should not be accepted, particularly for empowerment activities, because it interferes with self-reliance and leads to suspicions that the vested interests allegedly represented are motivated in ways counter to the true interests of the communities being 'helped'. In the case of India, the government has its own regulations with respect to foreign funds; it requires receiving organizations to be recognized under the government's Foreign Contribution Regulatory Act—not a foolproof instrument of control, since its intent can sometimes be bypassed by savvy and well-connected recipients, but a restraining factor against abuse, nonetheless. The groups discussed here do indeed accept outside funding, often significant amounts, no doubt realizing that without it their ability to operate would not support the critical mass needed for effectiveness. But they make sure that such assistance is consistent with their principles and priorities.

In fact, most of the leaders and movements described here have been supported by surprisingly few foreign donors. Because this form of empowerment is rarely susceptible to the prescribed project format generally preferred by aid agencies—it requires, instead, open-ended, long-term support of an ongoing *process*, and an overtly politicized one at that—most donors shy away from such undertakings. The mainly North American and European non-government organizations that might be most expected to assist appear to feel that their own financial contributors would not wish to be involved in what is perceived as a risky business; that they are inclined, furthermore, towards more visible humanitarian efforts. The problem is that what is often seen as humanitarian may not have humanitarian results in the form of justice for the oppressed. For this, political action to change power relationships can rarely be avoided.

The Context in Brief

Injustice is hardly new to India, or to the world. Over the centuries, wrenching stories of poverty, exploitation, violence and unparalleled human suffering have been the reality of life, and death, particularly for Dalits, tribals and women.* According to the Dalit Solidarity Network, there are 170 million Dalits in India, or 240 million if one includes those who have converted to Christianity, Islam or other religions. If one includes all scheduled castes and tribes, the number amounts to almost a third of the entire billion-plus Indian population. Up to 90 per cent of these people are said to live below the poverty line, comprising around 80 per cent of all Indians forced to endure this degrading lifestyle.

Aggravating the situation is the fact that Dalits have existed in conditions of apartheid for centuries, not allowed to cross the line dividing their part of the village from that occupied by caste Indians, not allowed to use the same wells, drink from the same cups of water or tea, or enter the temples. Where Dalit children

---

* The word Dalit is used throughout this book to identify the most downtrodden Indians in the current political terminology used by them; it means 'broken people'. Some readers will identify them by other terms such as 'outcastes' (since they are outside the formal caste system), (ex-)'untouchables' (their caste name), 'harijans' (Gandhi's term, meaning 'children of God') or 'scheduled castes' (the government's legal term under its equivalent of an affirmative action programme). While the real distinctions are no doubt more complex, the word 'tribals' in India refers to the country's original inhabitants who are said to have largely fled to the country's hilly areas at the time of the Aryan invasions, while other original inhabitants, who remained at lower elevations, are believed to comprise today's Dalits.

are fortunate enough to be able to attend school, they are often forced to sit in the back of the classroom, while their family members are likely to be malnourished, have access to a paltry share of arable land, and find themselves forced into demeaning forms of employment. The misery of the situation is multiplied in the case of women who bear the further discrimination accorded to their gender. The problems are most severe in rural areas. While millions migrate to seek employment and better lives in the exploding urban centres, other problems confront them there, including community breakdown as familiar environs and community supports are left behind.

What is encouraging, however, is the mounting, though certainly insufficient, attention being given to changing these conditions, and to doing so in ways that increasingly address the root causes, rather than merely the symptoms, of human suffering.

For all of India's oppressive poverty and overwhelmingly large population, the country's constitution and laws are among the most progressive in the world. This, and India's standing as the world's largest democracy, must be appreciated even as one is obliged to emphasize that the laws are observed at least as much in the breach as in reality. This is clear not only from the above observations, but also from countless stories told by movement leaders of cases ranging from economic privation, disenfranchisement and indignities (such as manual nightsoil scavenging), to more physically brutal atrocities and murders. All are rooted in the inability of poor people to achieve their rights under the law, rights of which they are often unaware in the climate of fear in which they, their families and caste members have lived for centuries. By some accounts, atrocities against Dalits have actually increased in recent years, with many afraid to report them, and government and police taking no action against offenders, describing these as 'social problems'. Here, indeed, lies the challenge to, and mission of, groups seeking change: to ensure compliance with the law for the cause of the oppressed.

Notwithstanding its progressive constitution and laws, India's government, like most governments, is not monolithic. The very enormity of the country, literally a sub-continent, would seem to assure that. Add to this the vastness of the government bureaucracy, especially given the historically large public sector mandated by post-Independence socialist policies, and it is clear that all manner of attitudes can be found represented, some willing to be sympathetic to the needs of the oppressed, and some less so, or not at all. The fact that those employed in government are generally considered, almost by definition, among the relative 'haves' in society also suggests that they may not be fully aware of the suffering that is part of daily life for so many hundreds of millions of their fellow citizens. Notwithstanding the pro-poor laws on the books, it has tended, furthermore, to be the better off, better connected, better educated, higher caste—in short, the elites—who have been most able to press their claims of government—to 'work the system'—at the expense of the poor. In short, there is a contradiction between the official laws and policy of the government and the reality of the society and bureaucracy within which it must operate: the latter inevitably demonstrating the power of the 'haves', and the former the necessity of equal rights, and power, for the 'have-nots'.

On the economic plane, recent years have seen a loosening of India's socialist, public sector-oriented economy, general economic and technological growth based on capitalist openings, and the dramatic growth of a prosperous middle class. India is now among the world's largest industrial powers and a member of the nuclear 'club'. However, economic liberalization and the forces of globalization have created a momentum that is often further antithetical to the interests of the poorest groups. As public sector enterprises have been privatized, government affirmative action rules no longer apply; it was these that were largely responsible for opening new employment opportunities to Dalits and tribals. As globalization has brought more foreign investment and more industries being owned by conglomerates, organizing the poor has become more difficult because there is no clear opponent on whom to focus and with whom to bargain. As more use is made of technology, as opposed to labour which India has in over-abundance, workers—especially the unskilled—have been displaced. Additional jobs have been lost due to increasing amounts of cheap imports—a boon for better off consumers but not for poor Indian workers. While some benefits from the new economy have no doubt trickled down to increase opportunities for some of the poor, one cannot deny the several trends that conspire to disadvantage them, thus further enlarging the gap between rich and poor.

On the social plane, countervailing, negative forces are at work in the form of increasing materialism, cynicism and brazenness among the members of the new middle class. In the words of one movement leader, 'the middle class has failed in this country; where its role was to transfer from feudal society to democratic society, it has become so selfish'. Indeed, these attitudes seem to be increasingly absorbed by the poor as and when they are able to progress; a number of references are made to 'dalit Brahmins'—those who, upon finally achieving success, become blind to their caste cohorts left behind. Meanwhile, in politics, the post-Independence national consensus has broken down, with the decline of the ruling Congress party and the rise of regional and coalition parties and politics. The historic pro-poor influence of Mahatma Gandhi has become marginalized and dissipated. In the words of a Marathi saying, 'the guards have changed, but the prison remains the same'.

Having said all this, certain positive trends may be observed. Most notably, the conditions for movements such as those led by the groups described here are believed to be better than before. The groups themselves have learned a great deal over the years and can now operate with improved capacity and greater effectiveness. The government's recognition of the role of non-government organizations has increased substantially. And the media are more responsive to publicizing NGO efforts and the underlying injustices that need correction. Finally, there are positive aspects of economic liberalization in the form of deregulation on which the poor can capitalize, and of globalization in the sense that communications technology now makes possible not only intra-India but also international publicity regarding human rights violations; indeed, a respected and reasonably powerful human rights institutional infrastructure now exists to lend support to India's struggle.

The first five chapters that follow offer illustrative stories of the types of situations these groups encounter, selected activities in which they engage, and accounts of how they carry them out. While traditional *development projects* are often part and parcel of their work, they are subsidiary to the major effort which can only be described as the *process of empowerment*. By reading their stories, it should also be possible to understand these groups' definition of empowerment—one that goes beyond the increasingly common rhetoric where, like the terms 'participation' and 'development', words are much bandied about but not always commonly interpreted and acted upon. Chapter Six reports on some variations on the theme, illustrating one organization's difficulty in shifting from traditional development approaches to empowerment, another's unique progression into a very different response to poverty and oppression, and others' application of the empowerment approach in responding to disasters such as the devastating 2001 Gujarat earthquake. Following these illustrative accounts, and based on the movement leaders' collective reflections and analysis of their experience, Chapter Seven brings together the major points raised, analyses the issues, delves somewhat more into the social, economic and political settings, and summarizes the lessons they have learned.

Chapter Eight, for both substantive and symbolic reasons, follows the previous format in telling the story of the Unitarian-Universalist Holdeen India Program (HIP) as a partner to all the groups described. The earlier chapters have purposely not dealt with donor issues in order to maintain appropriate focus on the groups themselves. But if the Indian leaders' lessons are important to worldwide understanding of how to promote development with human rights, HIP's lessons, corroborated by its Indian partners, have equally critical, indeed dramatic, implications for donors of foreign assistance. All have their roles to play in the struggle to end poverty and promote social justice.

Chapter Nine brings together the two themes of empowerment and donor roles in some concluding thoughts. Basic background information on each of the Indian groups whose story has been told, along with a list of organizations participating in this analysis, are conveyed in the appendices. The profiles of the organizations are given in the order in which they appear in the book.

Of Pigs and Goats
and Human Bondage

Vidyullata and Vivek Pandit wanted to work with poor people and bring change to their lives. Raised in Mumbai, they had been involved in organizing youth in urban slums through the Socialist Youth Movement. But the cry was to go to the villages because, as Vivek later wrote, 'India lives in the villages. When we went and started work, we knew some of the platitudes—people have health problems, education problems, they are poor because they have very little income. And therefore we responded in the mainstream manner.' They went to a village where Vivek had family; they offered pre-school classes for the children; engaged friends who were doctors to provide healthcare services; and organized income-generating activities such as pig and goat rearing. 'The entire village—men, women, children, from all communities— welcomed us with open arms because we were the first educated persons from Mumbai who had started "social work" in that area. The upper caste landlords as well as the tribals, everyone participated in our programmes. Indeed, it was like a family.'

A year later, the 'family' was to come in for a rude awakening.

Once we decided to organize a games tournament for the youth from the nearby villages,' Vivek wrote, 'and we started regular practice sessions in the evenings. My wife Vidyullata was very upset that some of the star players were very irregular in the practising. One day she asked them, "Why can't you come to play games in the evening?"

"Because we have to work for the landlords," they answered.

"Why don't you come in the evenings?"

"We are not free in the evenings, or at any other time, especially in the peak agricultural season."

"Why is this so?"

"Because the landlords had given money for our marriage."

We were horrified to learn that this was the life of labourers who were bonded to their masters for the life. Their wife and children, sometimes even grandchildren, were bonded to the landlords for a paltry sum of money taken for marriage or illness. For the first time in our lives we were coming across the very concept of bonded labour. We were so disturbed that our lives and thinking seemed to have been thrown out of orbit. We were shocked that we were living in a village where the tribals were slaves. It shook me that I had visited this village since childhood and was often carried from the bus stop to home by the tribals on their shoulders. That single conversation had changed our worldview. The idyllic rural setting now seemed oppressive. The myth of a homogeneous community was broken in our minds.'

'As long as we did not talk about bonded labour, the landlords treated us well. Indeed my own uncle was one of the landlords who owned bonded labourers in the village; I thus belonged to the family, caste and class of the masters. However, the moment we started saying that keeping bonded labour is an inhuman practice, some members of my own family turned against me. The interest of the owners was not in the money that the labourers owed them, but in having someone to order about for all kinds of work around the year. Their interest also lay in the social prestige; the more the number of slaves owned by a landlord, the greater his prestige and the tremendous feeling of power that one derives in playing God to other human beings.

Exploitative class relations are hardly new in the world but, as the Pandits learned, understanding powerlessness is the greatest challenge for organizers. Power relations may be so diffused as to defy immediate identification or quick solutions. This is why the Pandits came to understand the situation only after a year of working in the village and after talking with the bonded tribal youths. 'They were our first teachers,' says Vivek, going on to add, 'all that we were doing had nothing to do with the reality of tribal people's lives. Of what use were pigs, goats and pre-school classes if people were not free?' They decided they would do nothing else until the bonded labourers were free, and temporarily closed down their development activities.

It took two years from that point for Vivek and Vidyullata to first convince the bonded labourers that they *could* become free; the labourers had never thought in those terms. The power system was so infused into the society and into its behaviour patterns that, notwithstanding the democratic thrust of India's constitution and laws, it had gained social sanction. Oppression was thus systematized and rationalized in such a way that it remained unchallenged without conscious effort.

'Why,' asks Vivek, 'are the voices of the people not heard?' Because they lack power, of course. 'Power can be derived from social status, wealth, political connections or muscle power. But the people we work with have none of these, therefore obviously their voices are not heard. They have no power to bargain with the government or the oppressors because they have no leverage. The only potential of the masses lies in their vast numbers.' Yet caste, religion, language, regional and party divisions often prevent them from coming together as a common force, even if they could find a way to put aside the hopelessness instilled in them by centuries of oppression. They are steeped in a 'culture of silence', having lost their confidence, their capacity to dream, to hope.

Organizing as a common force—persuading the tribals to become free—was clearly the only way out of the vicious circle. But it was hardly an easy process. 'The landlords were angry that we were campaigning against them,' says Vivek, 'and the tribals ran away whenever they saw us because my uncle was a bonded-labour keeper. They thought we were the agents of the landlords. We were frustrated and were losing heart.'

Then one day we were attacked by the landlords. Our belongings were thrown out of our rented house. We had nowhere to go. That night the tribals took us home and dressed our wounds. They realized that we were with them, and since then we have remained with them. The relationship was strengthened when we registered offence against my uncle. Bonded labour exists not because of them but because of us. We can work with the bonded labourers for their release only when they are convinced that we are ready to be with them, and we are ready to risk everything, including our lives, to remain with them.

Freedom comes from countering power with power. Only by building the strength of the bonded labourers can their voices be heard, not only heard but acted upon. Our task is to help them through this difficult transitory period when they have no support and no help. This is always the testy period. Once we overcome this, victory for them is answered. A bonded labourer does not become free overnight. In this period of transit we have to help them in every possible way. Social legislation by itself cannot destroy slavery. While powerful laws are important and useful, without an insistent and equally powerful voice to demand their implementation, laws have remained on paper. Similarly, any other tool, like using the media, public interest litigation or using legislative devices, has to be linked to collective action if they are to bring long-lasting change in the lives of the people.

This commitment and readiness to take risks is often missing,' Vivek goes on to say. Commenting on the work of well meaning outsiders, he says,

I have seen NGOs who purport to release bonded labourers in India, Nepal and elsewhere, but whose paid staff are keepers of bonded labour, or whose orientation is against any kind of risk taking. Sometimes I come across NGOs that have made a project of releasing bonded labourers, and their activities include savings and credit, literacy classes, alternative employment, and so on. I feel that if voluntary agencies react to their poverty and illiteracy instead of strengthening them for release, then they too do not hold out any hope for those in bondage. How can people whose entire time from sunrise to sunset is owned by another come for literacy classes? And how will literacy help them? How can those who earn only in kind, and just enough to keep body and soul together, put in savings? Why should they save to buy their freedom when the law abolishes bonded labour? Once we calculated the amount that a bonded labourer would have earned if he were a free labourer, and we found that actually the landlord owes him money instead of the other way around. So why should a bonded labourer save to pay off an imaginary debt?

Releasing bonded labourers is not a project,' says Vivek, referring to the framework used by most donors who undertake development activities. 'It is entering into the politics of tilting the balance of power in favour of the marginalized. This requires knowing the various democratic institutions, the laws, and the pulse of the people, the mind of the opponent. But once bonded labourers are free, the sky is the limit. They do not wait for alternative employment or rehabilitation packages. Freed bonded labourers in Thane (our district in Maharashtra) have helped other bonded labourers all over the country in their struggle for freedom. They have even collected one rupee each as a token contribution to the freedom struggle of the African National Congress. They have truly understood in their hearts that no one is free till every one is free.'

During the period of India's independence struggle, Mahatma Gandhi once wrote that the British would rule India only as long as Indians allowed themselves to be ruled, an observation extended by Vivek Pandit to apply to oppressed peoples throughout history and around the world. Through his and Vidyullata's establishment of a rural development trust called Vidhayak Sansad, and its allied union Shramjeevi Sanghatna, they worked to change the mindset of the defeated people, so that they would refuse to play their role in accepting oppression. As a first step, the Pandits felt that it was important to give the bonded labourers a 'taste of victory', however small, so that they could see that it was indeed possible to win. To do so, they needed to provoke the people to analytically look at their own situation. Vivek offers an example of the type of simultaneously probing and sympathetically needling conversations he frequently has.

Vivek Pandit: Which village are you from?
Villager: Shimpala.
VP: Why have you come here?
V: To see you.
VP: Why?
V: Give us something.
VP: What can I give you?
V: Wheat.
VP: Why wheat? Don't you have enough work?
V: We work on others' fields. Our lands have been taken away.
VP: Who has taken your lands?
V: The village Patils.
VP: What do you mean? How did they take your land?
V: We used to plough the grazing land. The lands of the Patils were close to ours. So they threw us out. They threatened to kill us if we returned.

VP: So what did you do?

V: Nothing. We are poor. What can we do?

VP: Why don't you just enter into your land and take it under your control?

V: We will die. They will kill us.

VP: Actually you don't need the land.

V: We do!

VP: Why?

V: We have children. We have to feed them.

VP: So what? What is your caste?

V: Matang. Mhang.

VP: Then agriculture is none of your business. Mhangs are only supposed to play the traditional instruments. You are supposed to only work for the Patils and protect the village. Why do you ever want to plough the land?

V: We have nothing to eat.

VP: So what? Doesn't the Patil throw you something to eat every day? Enough to keep you alive?

V: We have no electricity.

VP: Now you start talking about electricity! Who said you needed electricity? You are cattle. You don't need electricity for your sheds! You don't want to be beaten, but you want your land. That is impossible.

V: We want the land.

VP: Go and possess the land.

V: But they will kill us.

VP: Can they kill all the forty-four of you? Otherwise leave the land, forget it. If you want land, get ready to die for it. Go and plough the land. If you cannot do it, then continue to play your traditional instruments. Let the Patils plough the land.

Then another villager spoke.

V: We are not cattle. We are also human beings.

VP: If you are human beings, then you should say, 'I will plough the land, and die'.

V: We will plough the land. We are human beings.

The very next day the Dalit villagers started tilling the grabbed land. The landlords reacted by attacking them and registering complaints with the police, but the Dalits did not let go their possession of the land. Even today, all 44 families plough their own land. The villagers had begun to organize.

Organizing, as defined by Vivek, is,

> a process that takes people towards a better tomorrow by saying 'no' to the present exploitative order. It begins by articulating a vision of a just society. It involves taking up issues of immediate concern to the community, and working in a planned manner on the issues, thus moving in the direction of the vision. It brings the marginalized people to the centre of the process by developing and nurturing community leadership. It also seeks and makes space for support from friends outside the community. It nurtures democratic functioning by taking people into confidence, increasing their self-confidence and self-respect. It increases the bargaining power of the people by realizing the potential of non-violent, direct mass action.

Organizing for empowerment is no easy undertaking. Institutionalizing the *capacity* to organize is even more challenging. It requires an extension of the original charismatic leader's ability to understand the local situation and inspire action. The Pandits are well aware of this and believe that they have created institutions which will continue even without their personal presence. This belief has been proven true for short periods, but has not yet been tested in a longer absence.

Vidhayak Sansad and Shramjeevi Sanghatna share a pleasantly shaded, peaceful campus amidst the low hills of Thane district, some two hours by road from the bustle and fumes of Mumbai, in the state of Maharashtra. Visitors are immediately struck to find themselves greeted not by the traditional Indian *namaste*, a greeting with hands pressed together as if in prayer, but by a clenched and raised fist, albeit good humoured, and a cry of 'zindabad!' that conveys commitment to victory. The greeting is emblematic of the conviction and determination of the movement's members.

It started with Vidhayak Sansad, which the Pandits founded in 1979 as a non-government trust working for the economic and social rights of bonded labourers and other oppressed and marginalized people, notably tribals, Dalits and women. In 1982, they registered Shramjeevi Sanghatna as a trade union primarily composed of agricultural and other informal labourers, including thousands who were formerly bonded. Funded by union dues, the Sanghatna fights, non-violently, for fair wages and other rights of exploited people. These two organizations are mutually supporting, essentially co-organizations—the first, a training and support-oriented NGO and the second, a people's struggle union. They share a combined mission, have partially overlapping staff and work with the same communities in the same geographic area. Subsequently, other bodies were created to serve particular, allied purposes—an advocacy group called Samarthan, in 1993, and a research and analysis department named the Centre for Budget Studies, in 1997. Vivek Pandit also played a major role in the creation of the National Centre for Advocacy Studies, to strengthen the capacity of social action groups around the country. Within his own state of Maharashtra, he and his colleagues have supported more than a dozen localized grassroots groups, notably in the Marathwada region. All in all, tens of thousands of people are involved in these endeavours—15,000 people are members of Shramjeevi Sanghatna alone.

When undertaking any activity, Vivek and his colleagues first ask, 'What will serve the needs of the poorest of the society?' and 'How does it fit into the struggle?'—questions that are not normally addressed by project-implementing NGOs who fear the risks of political engagement. Vidhayak Sansad's political engagement, however, is of a very particular sort. If radical in the sense that it challenges existing power, as it must in order to achieve power for the hitherto oppressed, Vivek's approach also has a kinder and gentler dimension, including the use of humour on occasion and celebrations to mark victories. The latter are particularly important, not only to acknowledge accomplishments, but to consolidate group solidarity and set the stage for further collective action.

In undertaking a particular activity or cause, emphasis is placed on finding allies in a position to help. 'In our struggle,' says Vivek, 'we have met the most feudal-minded bureaucrats, but we have also met many that have put their careers at stake to support the cause of the bonded labourers. There are politicians, media persons and judges who have helped us in many ways. Thus, there are many persons in the system who are sensitive to the problems of the people. Without their support our organization and we could not have achieved what we have.'

Vivek identifies three types of people to whom one must appeal—friends, fence-sitters and opponents. He observes that without friends, one is isolated; fence-sitters may be attracted to one's side and can become friends; and opponents are 'always fewer than us and also more powerful; the more united we are, the better are our chances for winning.' Vivek is careful to use the term 'opponents' rather than 'enemies', since the obstacle they present is one of policies or positions held rather than of their whole and personal beings. This distinction creates the possibility for them to be won over, as has happened in a number of cases through a combination of knowledge of the law, careful reasoning, strength of conviction and, no doubt, an element of charm.

In recent years, Vidhayak Sansad and Shramjeevi Sanghatna have placed increasing priority on education, noting that according to (probably understated) government figures, tens of millions of children in India receive no formal education—well over two million in Maharashtra alone. Many of them do not attend school because they are employed as labourers to help support their families, even though the Supreme Court of India has ruled that primary education is a fundamental right required by the Constitution, that where children are employed as labourers they cannot be obliged to work more than four to six hours a day and that, in such cases, they must be provided education for at least two hours per day, the costs of which are to be borne by the employer. Not surprisingly, the law is mostly observed in the breach, and Dalits and tribals, and girls of all groups, who are the most affected, are typically not organized to demand their rights. The situation is exacerbated by the fact that the traditional caste system invested the right to learning only in male Brahmins and upper castes, conveying social sanction for the educational disenfranchisement of others.

In organizing marginalized communities to demand their right to primary education, Vidhayak Sansad and Shramjeevi Sanghatna use examples from stories in the *Mahabharat* and the *Ramayana* to illustrate and motivate the people against the discrimination perpetuated against them. They point out that the government, in refusing to implement a substantial scheme for universal education, is reinforcing age-old discrimination and disobeying the Constitution and related Supreme Court rulings. The campaign for primary education thus becomes not just a matter of schooling but a broader demand for justice and equality. The execution of the campaign is also an example of how empowerment and development approaches may come together for optimal effect.

In the mid-1990s, Vidhayak Sansad and Shramjeevi Sanghatna began operating *bhonga shalas* ('shack schools') for children of migrant tribals working in brick kilns in Thane district. The teachers were youths, mainly tribals, from the local communities, rigorously trained for three months by Vidhayak Sansad. They used the government's village school curriculum, but with innovative teaching methods 'to make the learning joyful', as they put it. The history of the initiative is replete with attempts to gain government cooperation and resources to cover the costs of instruction, yet the government response was a lack of significant cooperation or even complete silence. A 1995 protest rally by women and children and a petition to the National Human Rights Commission led to limited cooperation, but the state government subsequently banned the employment of child labour at brick kiln sites on grounds of hazardous working conditions. Although this may not have been an altogether unreasonable decision, it certainly did not help assure the children their right to education, not to mention that (if implemented) it threatened their income-earning capacity At one point, Vidhayak Sansad conducted classes for child labourers at the office of the district collector, after brick kiln owners refused to give space at their work site for a school. Again, limited steps were taken when the matter was brought so visibly to government attention; but obstacles continued to be placed in the way of real support for the children's schooling, and the necessary funds were not provided.

When the government formally proclaimed that it did not have sufficient funds for rehabilitation of child labourers, and because Vidhayak Sansad had no funds left of its own to pay teacher salaries, they decided to organize the children to go with begging bowl in hand to the legislative assembly and to the homes of ministers to collect charity for the Chief Minister's Fund. This tongue-in-cheek event served as a photogenic opportunity for media attention and widespread publicity for the cause. Sub-sequently, the child labourers and Shramjeevi Sanghatna activists met the chief minister at his office and offered him a cheque for Rs 1,033 (US$ 23); he refused the cheque but announced the formation of a task force to study the educational needs of vulnerable children. Again, nothing happened afterwards until another demonstration was organized. The task force was finally formed eight months later, with Vivek Pandit as one of its members.

At this point, Samarthan, Vidhayak Sansad's advocacy affiliate, took a lead role in the activities, involving other NGOs working in education to join in discussing the scheme proposed by the task force, and urging political parties to include universalization of primary education in their party manifestos in advance of the upcoming legislative assembly elections (two of them did so). Eventually the government gave assurances on the floor of the assembly that the task force's final report would be implemented—but, yet again, nothing happened. In another creative and photogenic ploy, Shramjeevi Sanghatna activists and others initiated an 'agitation with blank slates'. Children marched in the streets carrying blank slates in one hand and the national flag in the other to demand implementation of the task force scheme. They also took along some goats on their march to symbolize that the government was still compelling children to graze goats rather than enabling them to attend school. Since the media were by now enthusiastically publicizing these colourful events, the government was obliged to respond, but did so, on closer examination, with a much diluted education plan. Again, Samarthan leapt into the fray, highlighting the problems and organizing the children to lobby legislators. In December 2000, a group of some 200 children knocked on 198 legislators' doors, from 7:30 to 10:30 in the morning, urging changes in the government plan. When offered sweets, some of the children replied, 'Sir, we want education, not sweets'.

In March 2001, the state of Maharashtra's highest education officials visited the *bhonga shala* schools, pronounced them 'path-breaking' and agreed to provide 1 million rupees in the current budget for them. In May, in what is said to be a first for India, a state government resolution established the Mahatma Phule

Education Guarantee Scheme for 6–14 year-old child labourers and other out-of-school children in the state. Noting that because many rural children work in the fields, in cattle grazing, sugar plantations or brick kilns, and many in destitute urban slums are wage labourers, rag pickers or domestic servants, innovative alternative education must, and will, be provided. Further, to ensure that actions follow words, local citizen's groups and NGOs are being enlisted to monitor the implementation of the scheme and hold the relevant local officials accountable for it. Perseverance has paid off, though the struggle for the right to education will no doubt continue.

One can hardly visit the groups' Thane campus without finding one or another cause being pursued. Indeed, Vivek argues that a struggle movement must constantly find new causes and new activities to ensure a necessary level of energy, and thus power, to face new challenges as they arise. On one occasion, two slick yet obviously harassed-looking factory owners were being chased by a defiantly shouting and somewhat menacing crowd of workers pressing for the right to form their own factory union—they had been negotiating, apparently without success, under Vidhayak Sansad's auspices. As the owners were on the verge of being physically overcome, Vivek stepped into the fray and firmly but respectfully urged the bosses to meet the workers' demands—a useful case of 'good cop, bad cop' strategy, or so it appeared.

Vivek Pandit narrates another, more extreme case at some length in order to illustrate the organizer's role in both exposing and obtaining justice for atrocities against marginalized people.

The 'Facts' on Paper

On May 22, 1993, at 11:30 A.M., a Matang youth, Rajabhau Londhe, died under dubious circumstances while working at the well of one Chhagan alias Sangeet Pawar, who belonged to the upper caste community. The incident occurred in Javla Khur village. Since Sangeet Pawar's well had remained dry even at 40 feet, he had decided to deepen it with the help of an electric crane. Electricity of the charge of 425 volts was available near the well. The driver's seat on the crane was wooden, the rest of the crane was made of iron.

On the fateful day (it was *amavasya*, or new moon), Sangeet Pawar and his mother, Vilas Bhakte, Laxman Mali and Rajabhau Londhe gathered at the well. Rajabhau Londhe was lowered into it in a trolley with the help of the crane. He died even before he reached the bottom.

The [report] recorded by the local police stated that Rajabhau Londhe saw a snake while being lowered and shouted, 'Snake! Snake!' and that the shock of seeing the snake caused his death. The same cause of death was indicated in the investigation too. The inquest, the post-mortem report and the statements of the witnesses all corroborated the story.

The 'Other Side' of the Story

On May 27, 1993 I [Vivek Pandit] personally met Shri Limbaji Londhe, the father of the victim. He told me that his son had been sacrificed by Sangeet Pawar to bring water to his well. He gave the following logic for his contention.

1) Before entering into the well, Rajabhau was asked to perform *puja* [worship]. Then his forehead was anointed with Kumkum. Thus, he was worshipped before being sacrificed.

2) *Amavasya* is not considered an auspicious day to begin any new venture, but this day is considered auspicious for sacrifices.

3) It is not important that the blood of the Matang should flow during the sacrifice. It is sufficient that he should die on the desired spot. Therefore, Rajabhau was killed by electrocution at the well.

4) The eldest son of a Matang is required for sacrifice, and Rajabhau was the eldest son of Limbaji Londhe.

The Beginning of the Investigation

The contention of the local police that Rajabhau died because of shock on seeing a snake in the well, and the contention of Limbaji Londhe that his eldest son was sacrificed, appeared to me as two extremes. I did my level best to investigate the matter carefully in an attempt to find out the truth. On the same day that I met Limbaji, I met the superintendent of police [SP] of Osmanabad, the [deputy] SP, the investigating officer, the medical officer, the police Patil, the father and brother of the victim—Shri Limbaji Londhe and Bhausaheb

Londhe—and also Shri Vishwanath Sitaram Kamble, one of the *panchas* (village headman) who was a witness to the inquest....

I studied the [various reports]. It was mentioned that Rajabhau shouted, 'Nag! Nag!' [snake, snake] before his death. In the inquest, some minor scratches along with three small marks on the feet and some injuries behind the feet are recorded. The report says that the inquest was completed between 5:00 and 5:55 P.M. However, according to Shri Vishwanath Kamble [it] was done between 7:00 and 8:00 in the evening. At that time the body had black and blue bands on the right hand and foot. [It] also informed that the fingers of the hands were close fisted. Since he is not literate, Shri Vishwanath Kamble did not read what was written in the report. [His] contention was supported by Viththal Bhagwat, Chandrakant Arjun Kamble and the brother of the victim, Bhausaheb Londhe.

Thus, there appeared to be a serious contradiction in the timings of the inquest. Also, [it] was completed in the light of a small bulb. Inquest should be done in clear light, and this simple rule was not followed.

Later I discovered that the black and blue bands on the hand and foot were not recorded in the postmortem report. The post-mortem report noted that both the hands and feet were stiff, and both the knees and ankles were also stiff. Death was reportedly to have been caused by the failure of heart and respiratory activity and due to shock. 'Cardio-respiratory failure due to shock.'

I read up the books on medical jurisprudence available to me and also consulted senior doctors. According to medical literature, shock is categorized into four broad types, and there are a total of 12 types of shocks. The deduction of mental shock is arrived at by the elimination of all the other eleven. The medical officer had only mentioned that the death was due to shock, but had not mentioned the type of shock. Therefore, the police had found it convenient to declare that the shock was due to the fear of seeing a snake. There was no elimination of the possibility that the shock was due to electrocution.

My Conclusions

Rajabhau was a young Dalit. Seeing a snake was nothing new to him. Moreover, every child in the village knows that water snakes are not poisonous. Therefore, it was highly unlikely that the fear on just seeing a snake would be so great as to kill Rajabhau on the spot. Secondly, according to medical sources a sudden shock can kill. If the shock of seeing a snake had killed Rajabhau, then it should have been a sudden shock, and he should have been dead before shouting out for help. It is also pertinent to note that just after Rajabhau was brought out, two persons, Vilas Bhakte and Laxman Mali, had entered the well. They did not see any snake in the well. They have stated this in their statement to the police.

Follow-up

I was convinced that the local police and the medical officer were trying to hush up the offence in an attempt to protect the culprits. I went even further into the investigation of the death and was able to prove that this was a case of murder and not a death due to shock. We demanded that the case be transferred to the Protection of Civil Rights Cell. Later the opponents got it transferred to the state CID [Crime Investigation Department]. I found that the case as framed was diluted by the state CID. They had not only dropped charges against the government officials; they had changed the nature of offence from murder to death due to negligence.

I approached the magistrate's court in a private case for registration of offence against the upper caste members accused, who committed the murder, and the government officials, including the police who covered them. This case was fought under the Scheduled Castes/Scheduled Tribes (Prevention of Atrocities) Act. The [Protection of Civil Rights Inspector General] was my witness. He took a great risk of his career and deposed against the police in the court. The magistrate upheld my argument and once again implicated the government officials, including senior police officials, and ordered the State CID to register the offence as a murder.

All in all, Vidhayak Sansad and Shramjeevi Sanghatna have won a number of victories. They have won land, other property rights and government rehabilitation support for thousands of families. They have won high court judicial reviews of questionable local rulings in specific human rights cases and promoted professionalism and accountability in the police forces and other government institutions. They have facilitated government legislative changes. Their direct and indirect influence in judicial, legislative, administrative and law enforcement arenas is impressive. This has happened in large part because their campaigns are structured with the goal of broad institutional change in mind.

Vidhayak Sansad's and Shramjeevi Sanghatna's campaigns employ a double-pronged strategy of organizing. First, they articulate demands for legal and institutional reform, drawing on existing laws that are not being implemented. They are able to gain attention for their demands because of their numerical strength and visibility, on the one hand, and their careful homework on the issues, giving them credibility, on the other. Second, their approach to the problems of the oppressed is often highly creative and sophisticated, as the brief examples offered here suggest. As in a game of chess, they are able to see several moves ahead in ways that win over or out-fox the opponent. And they persevere.

Their accomplishments, to be sure, have not come without setbacks and pain. Vidhayak Sansad first confronted the state on the issue of the law on bonded labour in 1982, lobbying legislators, working the media and going to court. It took two years, till 1984, for the state government to admit the reality of bonded labour, and another 10 years until legislation was passed outlining procedures to enforce the abolition act that had been adopted 18 years earlier. Similarly, the Atrocities Prevention Act of 1989, intended to prevent human rights abuses against scheduled castes and tribes, was not enforced until Vidhayak Sansad and Shramjeevi Sanghatna campaigned on behalf of a Dalit boy who had been stoned to death by an upper caste mob for having taken shelter from a storm under the roof of a temple (temples traditionally being off limits to Dalits). Before the campaign, most police personnel were not even aware that the law existed. The Pandits and other movement leaders have themselves been attacked, imprisoned and threatened with death by those hostile to their cause. Such is the cost of promoting human rights.*

* For a firsthand account of Vivek's story, see Pandit, Vivek, *Fearless Minds: Rights Based Approach to Organizing and Advocacy.* Pune: National Centre for Advocacy Studies, 2000.

Remarks by Mr Keshav Nankar, Executive Director, Shramjeevi San-
ghatna, at the Presentation of the Anti-Slavery Award to Vidyullata
and Vivek Pandit in London, October 27, 1999.

Honourable Mr. Neil Gerrard, Member of Parliament, Mr. Chairman
and all our friends at Anti-Slavery International, Kathy Sreedhar,
Director Unitarian-Universalist Holdeen India Programme, our
inspiration Tai and Bhau [Vidyullata and Vivek Pandit], distin-
guished guests and my dear friends.

I am here as a representative of numerous bonded labourers who
have been freed, who are seeing and experiencing freedom and
dignity for the first time. I want to express our gratitude and sincere
thanks to Anti-Slavery International for selecting Bhau and Tai for
this prestigious award as they are the genuine supporters and fight-
ers for our struggles and sufferings. They have been responsible for
helping us transform our lives, moving from an animal-like existence
to a life of dignity. Because of them, we now know what it means to
be human and to have confidence in ourselves....

Today I am here in front of you, speaking to you, after travelling
thousands of miles. This is unbelievable considering who I was in
1983. Today I have the capacity and the confidence to address thousands of brothers and sisters. I am proud that today I can deal with
government officers at various levels. And if they do not pay attention to my community's genuine demands, we will protest and demand our rights. Furthermore, I have become actively involved in
the political process. I contested the elections for the State Assembly.
I teach my fellow farmers the latest, modern techniques of farming
practices. Looking back at my past I cannot believe my present today.
It seems unreal but it's not a dream, it is a reality born out of a lot of
pain, a lot of struggle and a lot of dreams put together.

I remember as a child, when I was six or seven years old, my
father enrolled me in the village school. I used to like my school
very much. I especially loved the singing, dancing, and playing.
But my father needed some money. He asked his landlord—for
whom he had worked his entire life—for some money. The landlord
gave him the money but took me in return. He asked my father,
'What would your child do in school?' and 'How will he feed
himself?' He said, 'Remove him from school, send him here to look
after my cattle and I will give him one meal a day.' That is how I

was taken out of school when I was seven years old and I was not allowed to study beyond my first standard.

I continued working with the landlord. I got married and my wife and I worked in the fields and at home. Through marrying me, my wife also became a bonded labourer to my landlord. From dawn to midnight, we used to fetch water, clean the utensils, wash clothes, collect firewood and remove cow dung. We also had to prepare the ground for sowing the seeds, transplanting the saplings, nurturing the plants, harvesting the field, and finally husking the grains. The other agricultural labourers, who were lucky not to be bonded, worked much less and earned much more than me.

Once, to earn a bit more, I went to work with another landlord. This angered my landlord. He sent his henchmen to fetch me. They brutally assaulted me and verbally abused me during the journey back to my landlord.

My wages were not sufficient to feed my family even once. My debt kept increasing. I was getting sucked into a whirlpool. As a result, I became suppressed, with no voice of my own. I wanted to break the shackles and get out of this misery but I could not see any way out. In 1983, I met a few workers of Shramjeevi Sanghatna, a trade union that had started mobilising bonded labourers and small farmers in the neighbouring areas. They built our confidence and our powers. They taught us to say NO and not to bow to any injustice. They gave us the strength to fight against all sorts of atrocities that have been committed against us for generations. The landlords troubled us in many ways but the Sanghatna members remained with us through all our sufferings and hardships. When we were beaten severely, they were there getting beaten with us. When we had no food, they starved with us. This is how our struggle continued.

Today, in our area nobody dares to keep a bonded labourer. We proudly run the village Gram Panchayat [local government]. I contested the assembly elections based on the credibility of Sanghatna, not on the power of money. I lost the elections but it is not the result, but the process that is important. I proved that a poor person once without any rights, suppressed beyond imagination, could also emerge stronger and exercise his democratic rights to the fullest.

Today I also do collective farming, along with the other freed bonded and agricultural labourers. The landlords who were keepers of bonded labour now come to me for advice on farming. This is not my story alone but a story of thousands of changed lives.

2

Reclaiming
the Human Personality

Martin Macwan has a gentle demeanour, but he is angry. While still in his twenties and working with the poor on economic and social issues in the state of Gujarat, he experienced a horror that explains why.

One traumatic experience in 1986 changed our lives. In Golana (Kheda District), the government gave 33 acres of agricultural land to a dalit cooperative. The government gave another three acres of land to dalits for housing, but this land was illegally used by the Durbars as a [grain] thrashing ground. This was the main issue of confrontation. On the morning of 25 January 1986, the members of the cooperative were attacked, 4 were murdered and 18 wounded. Their houses were burnt. We were shocked and shaken. We registered a case and fought in the courts. The legal battle took 1-1/2 years. We worked very hard with the witnesses, instilled confidence to simply narrate what they saw and not get intimidated by cross-questioning. Finally Kheda District Sessions Court sentenced 14 people to life imprisonment. The Supreme Court upheld the judgement in the case of 10 of the 14 and the remaining 4 were sentenced to 8 years.

What Navsarjan is today really has its roots in this experience. We were pained at the lack of unity among the dalits. Violence is systemic and it shows its ugly face when the status quo is challenged.

In normal situations of conformity, fear of violence is palpable beneath the surface. We realised that the politics of traditional dalit leaders only accentuated sub-caste identities and conflict. The only way to counter this is through a broad based organisation, democratically, and using the laws of the land. I learnt the hard way and realised that unless we are able to build strong local leadership, and that too from the community which has suffered discrimination, we cannot hope to fight the oppressive caste system and its manifestations. Those who have themselves experienced violence and discrimination have a different degree of sensitivity, commitment, and also anger against the injustice they faced. Identifying and working with such local leaders, men and women, is the key.

Although Gujarat is known as one of the most economically advanced states in India, 40 per cent of its rural population lives below the poverty line, and there have been a growing number of incidents of massacres of Dalits, violence against Christians, and communal riots. More than 70 per cent of the Dalits in Gujarat are concentrated in the rural areas, where agricultural landlessness is a major problem due to the widespread failure of land reforms. Where Dalits do have small, usually marginal lands, they tend to be particularly vulnerable to quixotic monsoons and saline soils. Dalits from these areas migrate in search of labour for as much as half the year, dependent on high-handed upper caste landowners who usually pay well below the legal minimum wage. They and their families also face other problems, such as the harassment of Dalit women and the lack of schooling opportunities for their children.

Psychological oppression is equally serious. In Martin's view, the status of these people has a lot to do with a deep sense of insecurity. While it is true that a Dalit has been president of India, it is also true that for too many others the sole source of livelihood is cleaning latrines and carrying away baskets of human excreta on their heads. In the state of Gujarat alone, the number of such scavengers is said to exceed 40,000, and is supposed to be more than 700,000 for all of India. Legislation makes their employment in such activities a punishable offence, but even after a high court verdict on the matter, and despite governmental denial of the existence of the practice, it continues. As Martin observes, the scavengers know that scavenging is a noncompetitive occupation—no one else will do it—which for them brings security. Anything else, including selling vegetables, which is non-scavenging, is highly competitive. They know that the competition they face in the non-scavenging sector is not in the areas of finance or competence, but more a manifestation of the caste mentality.

In short, the scavengers are in a catch-22 situation.

The same level of insecurity haunts the lives of farm labourers. In Amreli District there was social ostrasizing of Dalits over a period of 27 months. No one would employ them, no one would sell them anything, and no one would take a ride in a rickshaw owned by them. The reason was that Dalits complained to police against the high castes, since the latter had tampered with their water supply. Crops on lands of Dalits were destroyed, in the presence of a battery of policemen. This incident resulted in the suspension of 9 police personnel for their neglect of duty. On the social sphere the social boycott, a weapon used by the high castes has been proved hollow. The high castes feel demoralised at the fact they were not able to handle and counter the Dalit victory. Some have come to the Dalits and said they realized their mistake and apologised. The high castes at present stand divided. When the National Human Rights Commission recommended compensation for the victims, the government, though forced to recognize the reality of the boycott, was unwilling to implement the Commission's order. Navsarjan filed a class action suit and asked the government to take appropriate implementation steps.

Navsarjan has been described as the first self-consciously Dalit organization committed to fighting caste and community-based discrimination. In the first two years of its existence, a core team of its workers lived among the Dalits, trying to understand their situation and the psychology of fear within which they live. They concluded that fear of violence was more influential in keeping the oppressive system in place and forcing Dalits to conform to centuries-old social norms than the trauma of actual atrocities committed. 'Fear is a major obstacle to growth and development,' Martin has stated. 'Fear makes you weak, but once we come out of it with understanding and confidence, tremendous energy is released.'

Navsarjan spent more than two years studying atrocities against Dalits in 11 districts of Gujarat declared to be 'atrocity sensitive'. They examined the extent of atrocities—which range in definition from harassment to murder, their causes, the caste identities of the offenders, the police procedures and their style of response, and the implementation of various provisions under the Atrocities Act. They also interviewed police personnel in order to know their views on the issue. Beyond the specific findings, which had apparently never before been revealed in such a comprehensive way, was the importance of the exercise in consciousness-raising among both the authorities and the Dalits themselves.

> The poor and Dalits do understand that caste is coupled with political power and it is further linked with the caste psyche that is prevalent in all spheres of civic life. They therefore undergo the perils of systemic helplessness. [At the same time,] they are no longer so naïve as to lay blame for their miseries purely and solely on their fate. Their immediate needs are for survival and security. In this context, to expect them to support and work for a long drawn out struggle-oriented agenda for systemic social change, sometimes even at the risk of deprivation of their immediate needs, creates difficult dilemmas for them.

Navsarjan's mobilization strategy is based on the recognition that atrocities are not individual cases but are rather the product of a well designed social system—hence the need for collective action. 'Besides,' Martin points out, 'togetherness always adds to the confidence of the community. We saw marked results of this very soon. The opponents were taken aback by community involvement of a prolonged nature. As a strategy, the workers never missed the opportunity to drive the point home.' He goes on to say,

> In the course of the mobilization programme, the tussle with the vested interests, largely political, becomes inborn. These interests never like their empires to be disturbed. There is another problem of similar nature with the Dalits. The traditional caste leadership, if not handled properly, can get threatened and turn against you. As a strategy we always stay away from caste politics. While it is easy

for an outsider to stay away from caste politics, it is not so for those workers committed to social change and who are Dalits themselves. While working on such loaded issues, which requires guts and leadership skills, these workers do receive a respectful following. Whether one wishes or not, this does change the power relations.

One of Navsarjan's major challenges has been to identify and adequately train its workers to effectively interact with Dalit communities on land, water, minimum wage, scavenging and related issues. For Martin, the main criteria for selecting workers are literacy and anger—anger about the system, sufficient to instil a commitment to fight for the cause. In a setting of widespread unemployment, there is no shortage of applicants, notwithstanding the very low wage that Navsarjan is able to pay (half of that of a primary school teacher), although there are subsequent problems of staff turnover as some eventually find better paying jobs. Navsarjan also has a preference for building the capacity of local leaders, giving educated youth a chance to develop and grow within the organization. Most critical, however, is their emphasis on training. Navsarjan's training lasts an entire year, conducted to a large extent on the job. A number of its workers have credited it with having changed their own lives.

As they go about their assigned village communities, Navsarjan's workers must absorb a lot of frustration without losing sight of their larger objective. They take a beating from both sides—while in continuous conflict with state or high caste elements on the one hand, they also suffer psychologically, since the Dalit communities with whom they work, themselves being at great risk, are unable to provide much support to their efforts. Even the scavengers who remove excreta sometimes abuse the workers, who appear to be telling them to give up the only safe and non-competitive trade on which they can depend.

The plight of women workers is even more saddening. First, they have to struggle at home to be able to appear in public life (as men have limited their traditional place to the home); then, when they *are* allowed to appear in public, they are often looked down upon simply because they are women. At the same time, Martin notes, 'we have experienced that women tend to be more active and action oriented than the men. Women have played a very important role in the area to add to the community awareness.'

Mobilization of the oppressed must begin with the creation of consciousness. Martin asks,

> Whom do we hold responsible for the violation of rights? Do we believe that we have some rights or do we believe that there have to be favours? If we understand that there needs to be rejection of the system in order to reaffirm our self-respect, then are we ready to let go some comforts and individual privileges that the system has bestowed on us to keep us divided?

While reference to comforts hardly seems apt for these down-trodden people, the last question refers to government affirmative action programmes that reserve a substantial percentage of jobs for Dalits and tribals—programmes which have had important impacts, but that have also served, no doubt, to dilute pressures for more fundamental social change, and have thus divided the Dalit community (divisions often encouraged by non-Dalit political parties for their own purposes).

In raising such questions, Navsarjan workers are continually struck by the sense of hopelessness and fatalism they face. This is hardly surprising, given the range of frustrations at every level. For example, the land revenue code states that when Dalit land has been encroached upon, the district magistrate can free that land. Navsarjan gives the example, however, of the case of a Dalit who had been trying for 36 years to accomplish this. In another case, Navsarjan advised Dalits to take possession of a certain parcel of wasteland and till it; when they did so, however, the village revenue officer threatened them. Hundreds of cases of this sort, and worse, can be cited by Navsarjan workers.

Water-related atrocities are also common, when non-Dalits or government authorities wilfully prevent Dalits from fair access to both drinking and agricultural waters, even when sufficient quantity exists. For example, in one village in Dholka district,

> drinking water is provided to the village by a pipeline of a World Bank aided scheme. As usual for the Dalits, there is a separate stand post. The non-Dalits intentionally tampered with the water supply for the Dalits who silently walked a kilometer to the highway along which a pipeline was passing. There was a small leakage, and a small pool of water had gathered there. The Dalits started filling

the water from there. This perhaps did not satisfy the miscreants, who then put their buffaloes in the pool, thereby making it a muck leaving Dalits without any source of water to drink. There are five Dalit teachers in the village, two of them being women. They felt hurt by the fact that in spite of their position as teachers they were made to suffer like that. The scene for others would definitely be more difficult. The two women teachers then went to fill the water from the public water stand where they were severely beaten. Later the non-Dalits, the family members of the elected representative of the village, attacked the Dalit locality, broke open the doors, and beat up only the teachers, saying, 'So, you are educated, oh'. Dalits were then prevented from going to the police station [to enter a complaint].

Conducting a survey of 50 villages, Navsarjan confirmed that the problem was not the shortage of water but its unequal distribution. While complaints were registered and sometimes led to site visits by government authorities, these usually achieved nothing. It turned out that the latter would talk only to non-Dalits and village officials, not to the aggrieved parties; so they learned that there was 'no such problem'.

The primary role and contribution of Navsarjan has been to raise awareness and help build confidence in Dalit communities so that they may assert their rights. This has been accomplished by thorough surveys of the conditions in the concerned communities, knowledge of legal rights and of political and psychological realities, and by strength of resolve.

In contrast to Vidhayak Sansad and Shramjeevi Sanghatna in Maharashtra, Navsarjan is characterized as a membership association but not as a union. Martin believes this is the most appropriate institutional structure in his context, allowing for strength in numbers as well as ready ability to address issues across occupational and, more recently, caste lines. As a membership organization, Navsarjan is also able to offer benefits such as medical and life insurance, which adds immediately tangible appeal for those who may perhaps otherwise be hesitant to join.

Although Navsarjan began with a specific focus on Dalits, the accumulating experiences with intra-caste conflict, coupled with requests from other groups who observed the advantages of a sound legal strategy and approach, has led to a broadening of the membership. Non-Dalits must, however, first pass a cleverly devised test—they must be willing to accept a glass of water from a Dalit, thus demonstrating that they do not recognize the caste system and do support social equality. Over the years, Navsarjan has also placed more emphasis on gender issues and on empowering oppressed women.

It may be noted that nothing has been said here about providing for more traditional development needs, such as for schools, health clinics and agricultural projects. Martin recognizes that such activities have their place but that they are subsidiary to the larger purpose of the movement, which is to engender power for the oppressed as the foremost requirement for ensuring human rights and economic progress. At the same time, one cannot work for the liberation of bonded labourers and then see them bereft of work opportunities; they must have land to till, help in procuring the necessary agricultural inputs, or some alternative occupational support. Similarly, one cannot urge scavengers of human excreta to assert their right to a more dignified and healthier occupation without assisting them to find appropriate alternative employment.

In addition, access to basic social services, notably health and education, is also necessary. A question arising here is whether it is preferable for the movement to create its own schools, for example, or to insist that government schools be provided. While the former would likely result in better schooling, which would also transmit values of the dignity of oppressed groups, the latter is in fact the right of every citizen, and the government is duty-bound to provide it. Navsarjan is grappling with these kinds of decisions within the dynamic of its evolving approach to improving the lives of the oppressed.

Navsarjan is also grappling with optimal ways to structure itself in order to preserve its flexibility and potency, even as its reach has extended to 2,000 villages in the state of Gujarat. Managing growth without losing the personal touch and special commitment is not easy. Nor is it easy to ensure effectiveness and continuity without undue dependence on the involvement of a charismatic founder. In response, the organization has increasingly established the *taluka* (sub-district) level as the base for local action, with the Ahmedabad central office supplying the requisite back-up support.

Having said this, one must also note how difficult it is to resist responding to new demands from areas lacking local representation. If news arrives of a particularly gruesome atrocity in a region of the state which has no Navsarjan workers, their inclination is to immediately respond, help the local Dalits lodge a formal complaint and gather the evidence that will be needed in court.

As his psychological insights into the Dalit situation suggest, Martin is a leader who thinks deeply and analytically about oppression and how to overcome it. A Dalit himself, though he has been educated in Jesuit schools, worked with Jesuits and earned a law degree, he sees the contradiction between advantageous affirmative action for Dalits, on the one hand, and the phenomenon whereby such preferences may vitiate a commitment to overturn the caste system, on the other. He also sees that in a country as vast as India, one organization's efforts inevitably constitute but the proverbial drop in the bucket.

To expand awareness of Dalit issues, Martin took on a leadership role with a number of other groups in issuing a 1998 'Black Paper' in the name of a National Campaign on Dalit Human Rights. Issuing a 'cry of appeal' for Dalits' rights, the Black Paper challenged the government and the international community to fulfil the provisions of the Indian Constitution and the Universal Declaration of Human Rights. In doing so, it cited the words of the Independence-era leader of the downtrodden, Dr B.R. Ambedkar,

Ours is a battle
not for wealth or for power.
It is a battle for freedom.
It is a battle
for the reclamation of
human personality

In 2001, the National Campaign was pressing to include caste-based discrimination on the agenda of the year's United Nations World Conference Against Racism, Racial Discrimination, Xenophobia and Related Intolerance held in South Africa. As Martin and his colleagues noted,

The elimination of caste-based discrimination and violence against Dalits presents a severe and urgent challenge to those concerned with human rights across the globe, whether in UN human rights bodies, governments, human rights commissions, NGOs and progressive activists. This challenge is clear and non-negotiable for five major reasons:

- ◘ The severity of caste-based discrimination, related to descent and occupation, is on par with racism and apartheid, which the UN, international community and human rights community actively addressed and intensely combated.
- ◘ The scope and enormity of caste-based discrimination encompasses 240 million Dalits in India alone, and more than 260 million in South Asia.
- ◘ Existing national legislations to prevent caste-based discrimination in South Asian countries have not been effective due to poor implementation, which itself is the result of a lack of political will of the governments involved. In spite of the various legislations, implementing agencies and monitoring bodies constituted, severe discrimination against Dalits persists. In fact, such discrimination has only intensified in recent years as evidenced by the alarming rise in violent atrocities and mass massacres against Dalits.
- ◘ Caste-based discrimination also afflicts a vast population of Dalits in other South Asian countries, namely Bangladesh, Nepal, Pakistan and Sri Lanka. Marginalised communities in Japan (Burakumin), Senegal, Nigeria (Ozu), and Europe (Roma) also suffer from a similar kind of discrimination based on descent and occupation. All these communities, constituting an enormous section of the global population, also require urgent and immediate attention and action.
- ◘ Despite completing more than 50 years of Universal Declaration of Human Rights, the international community and the UN bodies have failed to adequately address this major crime against humanity.

The Government of India tried to block inclusion of caste on the agenda of the world conference and refused foreign visitors visas to attend a preparatory meeting on the subject in New Delhi. To Martin and his colleagues in the National Campaign, however, the UN Conference offered an opportunity 'to make visible to the international community the numerically massive dimension of the discriminated peoples, and the heinous nature and devastating extent of the discrimination practiced and perpetuated against the Dalits in South Asia and against similar communities around the world.

Redressing such injustices is clearly a fundamental goal of many of the empowerment movements described here. In the case of Navsarjan, its particular success has been due to its focus on the psychological bases of oppression, and on building up the strength and spirit of the poor to overcome their condition. Its staff have done so by learning from the people themselves, conducting careful, indeed exhaustive, surveys of local conditions and, believing that no wrong should go unrighted, by filing legal claims against every injustice. And now they are also seeking international recognition and support for the cause. They thus contribute to the beginning of a feeling of empowerment for the oppressed, a beginning that is followed up by continually suing for their just rights, freedom and, yes, reclamation of their human personality.

Press release from the Robert F. Kennedy Memorial Center for Human Rights, October 11, 2000.

**Dalit Human Rights Advocate Martin Macwan of India
Named Recipient of 2000 Robert F. Kennedy
Human Rights Award
Leading Campaigner on 'Untouchability' to be
Honored on November 21st in Washington**

Washington, DC—Human rights activist Martin Macwan, a powerful advocate against the practice of 'untouchability' in India, has been selected as the winner of the 2000 Robert F. Kennedy Human Rights Award. Mrs. Robert Kennedy and Senator Edward M. Kennedy (D-MA) will present the 17th annual award to Mr. Macwan at a November 21, 2000 ceremony. The ceremony will be held at the historic Senate Caucus Room in Washington, DC.

'The Dalit are a group of people who are subject to the cruelest forms of dehumanization,' noted RFK Human Rights Award Judge Lynn Walker Huntley. 'Martin Macwan and his organization constitute a force for positive change.'

Martin Macwan was unanimously elected to serve as the National Convenor of the Indian National Campaign on Dalit Human Rights. He is also the Founder and Director of the Navsarjan Trust, an organization that promotes the rights of the Dalit, the 'untouchable' caste of Indian society. As members of the lowest rank of Indian society, Dalits face discrimination at almost every level: from access to education and medical facilities to restrictions on where they can live and what jobs they can have. Under Martin's leadership, the Navsarjan Trust has been one of the leading organizations in the advancement of Dalit rights. Based in the west Indian state of Gujarat, Navsarjan Trust currently organizes Dalits in more than 2,000 villages to fight the practice of 'untouchability' and to improve their socioeconomic conditions. Martin himself is a Christian Dalit, and he has personally suffered both caste and religious discrimination during his life.

The 1950 national constitution of India legally abolishes the practice of 'untouchability', and there are constitutional reservations in both educational institutions and public services for the Dalit. Unfortunately, these measures have not changed the reality of daily life for most Dalits, and many Dalit children do not even complete primary school. As Indian President K.R. Narayanan, himself a Dalit, noted in his public address to the nation on the eve of Republic Day, January 25, 2000, 'these [Constitutional] provisions remain unfulfilled through bureaucratic and administrative deformation or by narrow interpretations of these special provisions.' The Indian government's own National Commission for Scheduled Castes and Scheduled Tribes acknowledged in a 1997 report that '[w]henever Dalits have tried to organize themselves or assert their rights, there has been a backlash resulting in mass killings of Dalits, gang rapes, looting and arson.' The 1999 Human Rights Watch report, Broken People: Caste Violence Against India's 'Untouchables', notes that caste 'has been called India's "hidden apartheid", [where] entire villages in many Indian states remain completely segregated by cast. National legislation and constitutional protections serve only to mask the social realities of discrimination and violence faced by those living below the "pollution line".'

'In my view, the most significant factor in selecting Martin for the award was the potential impact given the size of the Indian population—160 million—whose rights are being violated because they are Dalits,' said RFK Human Rights Award Judge Sergio Aguayo Quezada. 'The fact is that the Indian government has been able to evade its responsibility to uphold the human rights of the Dalit because of the indifference of the international community.'

The Robert F. Kennedy Human Rights Award is presented annually to individuals who stand up to oppression and often face great personal risk in the promotion of human rights. The award reflects Robert Kennedy's absolute opposition to tyranny and his belief in the power of individual moral courage to overcome injustice...

Note: Martin Macwan has applied the US$ 30,000 cash prize to scholarships for Dalit children.

3

Trunks of the Banyan: In Support of Women

The sun reflects off the white desert sand like a mirror, bringing with it the sweltering heat of summer in the Rann of Kutch. Few trees are visible on the flat horizon. The only motion is the illusory spectre of the melting air rising from the ground, rippling as it goes. It too is trying to escape the scorching heat of the sands. Nothing offers any shade.

Jamu is resting from her journey through the desert that started just after the sun began its downward journey in the sky. Her infant son is resting on her hip, sleeping from either exhaustion from the heat or lack of food, or both. His hair is bleached and dry from malnutrition and overexposure to the sun. Jamu's bare feet are crusted in salt, the mark of her trade—salt farmer. She lives and works in the desert eight months of the year, extracting the white grains in the white heat of the white desert.

Now she is travelling the six kilometres that lie between her mud hut in the desert and the nearest village, Patanka. In the village, she hopes to find the rice and millet she needs to feed her family. There is a government fair price shop (FPS) in the village, but there is no guarantee that they will have even the basic items she requires. In fact, they rarely do.

If not, then she will have to pay the Rs 4 bus fare to go to the next provisions shop. She makes 15 rupees a day, working in the salt pans. Today's trip will cost Rs 8. The food will cost Rs 15. The loss in labour for the hours she is gone will be Rs 5. She will have to borrow from the shopkeeper again. That means she will have to pay five times as much with interest, but her family has to eat.

She has to make this journey every day. The sand doesn't get any cooler. The distance doesn't get any shorter. The debt just keeps getting bigger.

Ten years later, Jamubhen Ahir is the chairwoman of the watershed committee in her village. When she wants extra income, and the conditions are right, she collects gum from the trees surrounding her village, where, until recently, there was only desert. Otherwise, she makes over Rs 700 a month doing embroidery in her home—her home with a concrete floor, a tile roof and plaster walls. The house is in her name, the same name as on her savings account. She buys her food from the Shakti packet shop near her house. It always has what she needs. Her son is married now, and her two young daughters, in a setting where daughters are not always welcome and nurtured additions to the family, have just returned from school. The girls are healthy and smiling.

Jamubhen is a SEWA member.

SEWA, Self-Employed Women's Association, was founded as a labour union in 1972 and is probably India's best known non-government organization. Beginning in the Gujarati city of Ahmedabad, its initial focus was primarily urban, its members women who worked in the informal sector, including vegetable vendors, *bidi* (small Indian cigarette) rollers, head-loaders (construction workers) and paper trash collectors—people who work for meagre wages, are highly vulnerable to labour market fluctuations and are the poorest of the poor. Women are particularly susceptible as victims of underdevelopment and poverty, of discrimination and violence. But they are also producers, workers and entrepreneurs contributing to the family and to the economy. In addition, they work as artisans, as factory workers, on family farms, as agricultural labour on other people's farms, in forests collecting minor crops and as livestock tenders.

The scale of women's concerns can be seen in the figures cited by SEWA. Among an overall Indian population of one billion, 92 per cent of the employment is in the informal sector where there is no fixed employer–employee relationship and thus no welfare benefits. These people, nearly half of whom are women, are the unprotected labour force of the country, though government statistics show that they contribute nearly 63 per cent of the gross domestic product. From the early 1970s, SEWA began to organize the street vendors of Ahmedabad. They report,

By the early eighties, the repression and eviction of vendors had become unbearable for our members. There were daily beatings by the police, demands for 'hafta' or pay-offs were increasing, and the municipal corporation's 'anti-encroachment squad' had played havoc with women's livelihoods. Their goods were routinely confiscated and rotted in municipal godowns, and their baskets and other work equipment were locked up for weeks. And so the women organised. Their union, SEWA, initiated dialogue with the local authorities and the police, organised satyagrahas (strikes), and finally approached the Supreme Court for justice.

When Laxmiben, Rajiben, Elaben, and the others testified in the Supreme Court, all they asked for was for 'two baskets worth of space' in the main market of Manek Chowk. They just wanted to be left to sell in peace. Fortunately for them, the Supreme Court ruled that either an alternative market be developed or that the status quo be maintained.

Today, Rajiben, Laxmiben, and others sell their wares in the market as their mothers and grandmothers have done for generations. From time to time they still have to face some problems, but by and large their right to work and work security has been safeguarded. And their struggle has had its spin-off effects.

The vendors' membership in SEWA has swelled. Vendor leaders have learned to negotiate with local authorities and even use the courts where required. Vendors from five other markets also secured their right to work and sell in the markets, without fear of eviction and the customary pay-offs.

And where has this right to work led? Street vendors have sent their children to school—there are even a few doctors and lawyers among them! They have organised child care for their children while they're out at work. And health care, including health insurance for themselves. Through their own SEWA Bank, they have saved, taken loans, and developed business. Some have even stood for political office! Others have developed as strong leaders within the union. Leelaben who was part of the first Manek Chowk struggle is now a video producer. And they have their own vendors' cooperative and now direct linkages with growers for better prices for both vendors and growers.

With their new-found work and income security, many vendors have invested in their neighbourhoods. They have joined hands with the municipal corporation and contributed from their earnings towards basic amenities—water, toilets drainage, electricity—in their neighbourhoods. They say proudly we no longer live in a slum but in a housing colony!

Whether in the cities or in its expanding rural work areas, SEWA's role is to empower women by means of the twin strategy of labour union struggle and development through income-generating activities. Perhaps because of the quietly charismatic personality of its founder, the diminutive, soft-spoken Ela Bhatt, or perhaps because their economic and social service activities are so visible, or possibly because it is so difficult to denigrate the good cause of motherhood, SEWA appears to be seen as less confrontational and 'political' than some of the other struggle groups discussed in this volume. 'Because of the social service activities,' says Elabhen, 'our members gained confidence in resisting the employers and remaining firm in their legal demands. The employers also are impressed by these services. They have vehemently opposed us in the village, in the factory, at the negotiating table, and in the court, yet many of them have been quite receptive to our social programmes. The very employers against whom we are fighting for labour rights in the court have allotted space, foodgrains, and financial support to our childcare centers!' SEWA's ability to balance its twin strategies is indeed exemplary.

In Jamubhen's situation described earlier, it was the government of Gujarat that invited SEWA to become involved. In her part of Banaskantha district, a foreign aid-supported pipeline project had largely failed to deliver water to the people; besides this, and partly, no doubt, because of it, the people in the area had no work. SEWA's challenge was to foster the local women's interest in changing this situation. They were living in an environment steeped in tradition, beneficial and worthy of preservation insofar as it embraced practical adaptations to a difficult environment, but destructive in its denial of nutrition, literacy and control of assets. The traditional way of life was such that the women often failed to recognize their deprivation. SEWA's task was to 'ignite a flame of interest in the women of the villages so that they recognize the need for change and the potential path to it. The first step,' according to the SEWA workers, 'is to inform these women of their rights. A great deal of time is spent just talking to the women about this one issue. These initial discussions can last hours, and often take several meetings in the same village before the women are moved enough to act. But the organizers possess the skill to convey their message and the patience to see their goal through. Organizing is a process that never ends.'

Another short story is further illustrative.

Rajibhen, from Garamdi village, is a leader on her village water committee. She recalls that before she became a SEWA member, the village water tap, connected to the pipeline, only worked about once every other week. There was a water committee, all men, but they never met. She jokingly looks at the men in the room listening to the conversation and chides them about their inaction on the issue. The men smirk, mumble and look at the ground for lack of a good response. As three buffaloes munch on substantial piles of fodder in her courtyard, Rajibhen talks about the situation 10 years ago. In those years she was forced to migrate with her family and cattle. The final year of the big drought, just before she joined SEWA, she left Garamdi with five buffalo and only came back with three. Two had died of starvation and thirst on the way to Saurashtra. This had constituted a major loss in income and assets.

Things have improved since then. Thanks to the organized efforts of the village women, and some men, the pipeline water comes twice a week. It is still not enough, but they can get drinking water from a few kilometres away. Their top priority is income, and their efforts in the Water as a Regenerative Input Program reflect that. They have focused on irrigation resources and contour bunding. With fodder through the women's association to keep their cattle healthy, milk production is strong. Combine that with the lush crops in their fields and they are busy in Garamdi. Now they do not have to migrate.

Rajibhen has taken a loan and purchased a new buffalo. She is confident she will get a return on her investment. With plenty of water and fodder, the buffalo gets ample nutrition and produces good milk. With income more secure, the village water committee is now making plans for a new watershed development project. Their neighbours in the village of Datrana have an agrifilm pond. People in Garamdi are in agreement that they want one too. They are already preparing to procure funds from among themselves and gather the technical inputs.

In both cases, through SEWA's leadership in organizing the Banaskantha women's group, members were able to draw direct benefits from available but underutilized government and foreign aid programmes. Too frequently, such schemes, planned and implemented from above, do not link up with grassroots realities, particularly those of the poorest people, notably women. With SEWA's organizing and technical support, and by working together, the Banaskantha women were able to increase their access to precious water by improving their rainwater harvesting techniques, primarily through check dams, land levelling and well improvement. They thus gained a year-round source of drinking water; an increase in agricultural production, from one to two or three crops a year on some fields; reduced health risks through better hygiene and sanitation; and a decrease in the time spent on procuring water for daily use (thus gaining time for income-generating activities). Taken together, the result was more work, increased incomes and healthier lives.

SEWA went further. When the workers first became involved in Banaskantha, they were struck by the quality of the embroidery nd patchwork done by the village women. 'The design and manu-acture of the rich traditional wear was executed with a skill that lurred the line between artisan and artist,' they observed. The /omen were conscious of their skill and proud of it. They knew it ad value. They just did not know how much. Clothing was nor-1ally made to be worn by the family members of the woman from /hose hands it came. When SEWA organizers indicated that the rafts might have commercial value, the women told them that ·aders occasionally came to the village and purchased their work ·om them. Through more discussion and investigation it became lear that the prices these traders offered the women were only a ny fraction of what the crafts were later sold for in the open 1arket. In fact, the traders often bartered for the women's andicrafts, offering steel and plastic vessels in exchange for nbroidery—exchanges that were heavily in the traders' favour. 1e women suspected that they were not getting the full value of eir product but did not have access to the craft markets. Nor did they have a strong perception of the tastes of potential buyers. When custom dictates that you cannot travel outside your village without an accompanying male family member, such perceptions are difficult to formulate. Thus began what is potentially the most monetarily fruitful programme in the Banaskantha project.

SEWA organizers collected the work of a handful of village women who were interested in expanding their potential, and paid the women for their work on the spot. They then identified a market for the goods in Delhi, which encouraged a few more women to join the enterprise. To facilitate the effort, and noting that it would benefit both the women's families and the community as a whole, support of the other villagers was solicited and received. Forming a membership organization of the participating women permitted assistance in the form of loans to be taken from government sources, monies that could be used for the purchase of raw materials, for training and for wages in the initial stage. Particularly important was training in quality control and finances, including fair pricing. Ultimately, more refined marketing systems were developed.

An impediment discovered along the way was some crafts-women's failing eyesight. This was due to poor nutrition, aging or inherently poor vision, exacerbated by the straining detail work of doing embroidery in poor lighting conditions (no electricity in some areas and single bare light bulbs in others). Responding to the women's need, eye clinics were arranged, with 1,000 women examined in the first year and 876 provided with prescription glasses.

Today the women are producing stunning crafts and art works, while bringing about a generalized rise in wage rates in the district. Analysis has shown that even the agricultural wage rate, the foundation of the local labour market, has risen in a way that suggests a relationship to the rise in artisan-based employment. With the craft programme offering wages as high as Rs 50 per day, wages for agricultural jobs sometimes rose to Rs 60 in order to lure women into the fields to harvest the crops before they could spoil.

Another illustration comes from the village of Vauva where most of the craftswomen are from the Aahir community. As SEWA staff explain, the women of the Aahir caste are traditionally not allowed to work outside of their home and never permitted to travel beyond the boundaries of their village. In 1992, the Aahir community held a regional Caste Panchayat (meeting) in Vauva. The only way in which the women were to participate was to cook and clean for the several hundred men who attended the meeting. However, at the time of the meeting the Vauva craftswomen were working hard to fill an order for their craft cooperative. As a result, the men of the community voted to ban the women from further participating in SEWA activities. Any exceptions the women were previously allowed were revoked, such as traveling to and from the Craft Center in Radhanpur to exchange raw materials and finished products or attend meetings. The women of Vauva refused to accept the decision. A leader among them arose and presented their case to the community leaders. Bhachibhen pointed out to the men that the work the women were doing was making a tremendous difference in their lives. There was no more need for migration during the droughts, since the work was unaffected by bad weather. The income for the families had risen significantly and with it health and nutrition had improved. The logic of her demands were ultimately recognized by the men and the ban was lifted.

Perhaps most important, however, as one SEWA member says,

> the women who are members of the craft programme have developed an independence that reflects, and even outshines, the strength of the organization to which they belong. Their confidence has increased as they have all ventured beyond the confines of their village, many beyond the borders of their state, and some to other countries. They have confidence that knowledge affords, knowledge in their abilities and their value.

Among the more explicit of SEWA's advocacy activities was its 'Clean Ahmedabad Campaign'. As a SEWA report put it, 'The poor in the slums especially, face piling of garbage, filthy and insufficient number of toilets, overflowing drains, stagnant pools and polluted drinking water, which spread disease and make their lives miserable. The public authorities alone are unable to handle the huge problems of the cities.' SEWA members, especially paper and rag pickers, got together with industry representatives and inhabitants of middle class colonies for the campaign, which went on to win a major national award given by the Federation of Indian Chambers of Commerce and Industry. Similarly, SEWA conducted a campaign for the recognition of *dais* (traditional midwives) in India. For centuries they have been conducting home deliveries and providing other health services, but without recognition by the government's health department and without being given the respect they are due and the training needed to improve their performance. In view of the frequent inadequacy of government health facilities, particularly in rural areas, giving traditional midwives the responsibility of providing proficient decentralized healthcare at women's doorsteps is both practical and desirable.

SEWA's balancing of union struggle and more traditional development projects is so integrated that it is virtually impossible to disaggregate the two approaches in daily practice. Members struggle and advocate against the many constraints imposed on women by society and, at the same time, strengthen women's bargaining power and offer them new alternatives through development activities. The Banaskantha case of women being paid reasonable wages for their craft production and thus landlords being forced to pay higher amounts for agricultural work is a good example of this integration. SEWA's development activities are little different from those of many other voluntary organizations, Indian or international. Small enterprise development, agricultural and water cooperatives, savings and credit associations, health and childcare—all these are typical activities of NGOs around the world. However, SEWA has attracted more government and international support through its activities than any of the other groups discussed here. What is different about SEWA is that it has placed these approaches and activities within a larger strategy, perhaps not as confrontational as those of Shramjeevi Sanghatna or Navsarjan can be at times (could SEWA's normally gentler tone be gender related?), but just as broad-visioned and determined.

What is also different about SEWA is the extent of its reach, emerging from the vision of Ela Bhatt and her colleagues. Over its nearly three decades of existence, a longer time span than that of any other group discussed here, it has embraced trade organizations that promote employment, increase income and link female workers and producers with the market; organizations that build assets through savings and credit, such as the SEWA Bank; and organizations that provide social security, defined in Indian terms as health and childcare. These organizations, in turn, operate at village, district, state and national levels. Structurally, they may be registered as cooperatives, societies, producer associations, or even remain unregistered. They embrace milk producers, artisans, agriculturists and forest producers, salt makers, vendors and cleaners, among others. It is a huge network, involving hundreds of thousands of women. Their common characteristics are that they are owned, managed and democratically run by the self-employed women themselves, and that they aim towards self-reliance, both managerial and financial.

The 'Ten Questions of SEWA', frequently cited by its leaders, shed clarifying light on their holistic philosophy and approach:

1. Have more members obtained more *employment*?
2. Has their *income* increased?
3. Have they obtained *food and nutrition*?
4. Has their *health* been safeguarded?
5. Have they obtained *childcare*?
6. Have they obtained or improved their *housing*?
7. Have their *assets* increased? (Assets such as their own savings, land, house, work space, tools of work, licenses, identity cards, cattle and share in cooperatives, and all in their own name.)
8. Have the workers' *organizational strength* increased?
9. Has workers' *leadership* increased?
10. Have they become *self-reliant*, both collectively and individually?

As movements grow and expand in influence, the question of the leaders' relationships with political parties inevitably arises. Elabhen says,

One of my early decisions was to keep SEWA out of party politics. This has not always been easy, but it has proved to be a wise decision. I do not believe that politics is bad, but personally I cannot and do not want to be a politician attached to any particular party. I have preferred to be empowered along with other women getting empowered so that we can become a force that all parties must acknowledge. We do want to be a political force as a voice for poor women. SEWA is a convenient body, or a medium, for government to deal with. I know they use us as an intermediary. In turn, we use the government and their resources for the sake of the poor. Any government that comes in power has to show that they are reaching the poor and women, so working with us helps them.... This is the kind of relationship SEWA has with the official power structure. We are sensitive to each other's agendas, and we collaborate with each other when we can. The best thing about the powerful officials is that they are not permanent. The bureaucrats and politicians are not in their offices forever, while we are!

SEWA today can be described as a family of institutions, somewhat in the same way as the Vidhayak Sansad network of organizations in Maharashtra, though SEWA-originated institutions tend to act more autonomously while still cross-pollinating and cooperating among themselves. As Elabhen has described it, they are like the banyan tree that constantly grows and sends out new roots of growth. 'Each leaf, twig, branch, trunk of the banyan survives on the other's sap. You may cut it anywhere, yet the tree will not die. A day comes when the banyan has spread itself wide and deep into a forest. You cannot find the original parent and there is no point in trying. How wonderful! That is my vision of SEWA. Each of its activities grows and takes root as an independent, autonomous organisation. Yet they remain interdependent, gathering more strength by working together.'

Two major institutions of the SEWA family are the Gujarat Mahila Housing SEWA Trust, which was established in the recognition that roughly half of the SEWA Bank loans went for housing purposes, and focuses on a range of housing issues; and the Friends of Women's World Banking-India, an international institution with which Elabhen has been involved from the beginning, and which has guaranteed over US$ 150 million in loans to 500,000 women in 45 countries; in India, it provides credit to non-SEWA members.

An important component within SEWA itself is the SEWA Academy, which provides training for union members and research for institutional planning purposes. Elabhen learned in her early days in the textile workers' union that independent data is essential to effectiveness. The academy therefore processes all the grassroots information and data which directly relate to the lives of SEWA members and uses this information and language to communicate with policy-makers. 'They know so little of the day-to-day lives of the working people of the country,' Elabhen notes, going on to say, 'the information we bring is important, authentic, and credible. It supports our campaigns for political and economic programmes'.

Another branch of the banyan tree is SEWA Bharat. Initially intended as a federation of SEWA organizations throughout India, it is now a structure that promotes organizations of home-based workers and carries out studies on national and international bases. In fact, Elabhen now spends a considerable amount of her time on international issues because, as she puts it, 'SEWA's agendas at home and internationally are thoroughly interlinked. Many local issues have national and international implications and vice versa. We just cannot afford to ignore them. Nowadays it is the international powers who decide our lives. It is the big world powers who decide what we eat for our evening meal: *roti* (wheat) or rice, what fibre we wear, what medicines we swallow, what language we teach to our children. All are decided far away from our homes, often in foreign lands.'

SEWA's international outreach has taken two major forms. First, it has advocated internationally for the types of groups with which it has gained considerable success. For example, a home-based workers' campaign started by SEWA in the 1970s reached its peak when, in 1996, the International Labour Organization (ILO) voted for a worldwide convention to accord them full rights as workers. Similarly, SEWA drew attention to the problems faced by street vendors who constitute an important but unacknowledged part of the urban distribution system, and are often treated as criminals. At a meeting in Bellagio, Italy, on 'Legal Rights for Street Vendors in Our Cities', an international declaration demanding vendor rights was passed. Equally importantly, international networks were strengthened through these initiatives to support on an ongoing basis vendors' and home-based workers' causes.

Second, SEWA's reputation has led to expressions of interest from other countries wishing to learn from and replicate its successes. Although SEWA's accomplishments in India undoubtedly owe much to the particular context of India's independence movement, favourable constitution and laws, as well as its history of strong unions, SEWA groups have now been formed in settings as diverse as South Africa, Turkey and Yemen. SEWA leaders in India believe their model can operate wherever a union or cooperative tradition exists, but add that the particular manifestation will no doubt vary from one setting to another. It is important, they say, to be flexible, pragmatic and non-doctrinaire; to mould the movement within the specific context of the local setting; and to move one step at a time in pushing the bounds of acceptability.

In South Africa, the SEWA-inspired Self-Employed Women's Union has several thousand members who have successfully struggled for vendors' rights and have obtained several policy breakthroughs with municipality and other local authorities in the city of Durban. Following a visit to SEWA by two Turkish women active in the women's and workers' movement in Istanbul, neighbourhood workers' committees are being formed in Turkey. Islamic societies might seem to present unfavourable conditions for such a committed women's rights movement as SEWA. Yemeni women, for example, had earlier been limited to meeting in private homes and gathering as 'sewing groups'. However, a delegation from that country, representing women working in such home-based activities as crafts, cane work and agricultural production, visited SEWA-India and subsequently registered their own membership-based workers' organization—the Women's Economic Empowerment Association. Thus, working through both national and international alliances, SEWA-India's leaders seek to improve recognition and rights for home-based workers around the world. 'Every step forward helps,' they say.

4

Struggle in the South:
Land to the Landless

Chennaiah was born some 40 years ago to poor, illiterate, landless labourers in the south Indian state of Andhra Pradesh. Inspired by an uncle who had succeeded in becoming a member of the prestigious Indian Administrative Service, he was able to overcome the typical limitations of his background and attend school. At school he was strongly influenced by a teacher who was involved with the Naxalite (Marxist–Leninist) party. In the mid-1970s, the teacher was arrested, and so were some of the students who had supported him; Chennaiah himself was in prison for nearly two months. After his release, Chennaiah gained a student leadership position in the party and soon found himself leading a hotel workers' strike—a strike which, he reports, succeeded in procuring some wage increases but failed on the whole. Becoming disillusioned over time with the undemocratic aspects of the party and the violence it practised, which often harmed innocent people, Chennaiah left to earn a law degree. At the same time, he channelled his concern for human rights by taking up the cause of agricultural workers through an NGO called Sahanivasa. Soon realizing that NGOs were unable to lead the level of struggle demanded by the situation, he joined with other like-minded groups in the state in a workers' federation called the Andhra Pradesh Vyavasaya Vruthidarula Union.

By 2000, with Chennaiah as general secretary, the federation had about 300 member unions and was spread throughout most of the districts of the state. Along with release of bonded labourers, implementation of minimum and equal wages and promotion of Dalit rights, a major objective of the federation is land reform. 'The Indian Land Reform Laws advocate radical distribution of land,' Chennaiah has written:

> Despite two rounds of land reform legislation in India, the surplus land acquired and distributed among rural poor has been less than 2 per cent of total cultivated area, whereas in other Asian countries,' according to his research, 'it has been 43 per cent in China, 37 per cent in Taiwan, 32 per cent in South Korea, and 33 per cent in Japan. The lack of political will leads to deliberate non-implementation of Land Ceiling Laws in several states of our country. In rural reality, if there is a small piece of land, it can serve not only as a supplementary source of income for a rural labour household, but also as a source of security. In other words, the land reforms empower the rural poor if they own agricultural land of at least an acre with water facility.

To maximize member power, and in common with other movement leaders, Chennaiah emphasizes the critical importance of knowledge—knowing local land records, ownership details, legal land ceilings and the respective strength of individual landlords and politicians; the last is critical in order to gauge their ability to fight union attempts to procure land for the poor. Chennaiah admits that if moves to occupy government land may seem to be technically illegal, the government is also operating illegally since such lands are meant to be distributed to the landless.

All too often, he recounts, it is the wealthier, influential people who monopolize the land. In one case on the Tamil Nadu state border, local union leaders managed to smuggle out of government archives an old map showing that a landlord had been illegally given a certain piece of agricultural land. A group of low caste union members, living in such poor circumstances that they had little to lose, then occupied the land. The landlord burned down two of their huts in retaliation, causing a number of the occupiers to flee for safety. Others courageously remained, no doubt encouraged by the legal support provided by the union organizers, telling visitors that the prospect of having their own land, and the resultant pride and security of owning an asset, helped them overcome the fear of more landlord wrath.

Chennaiah and his colleagues tell the story of Anantapuram complex, a village of landless Dalit families and a few cobblers:

All the families earn their bread by working on the lands of the landlord as agricultural workers. They are paid Rs 20 (US$ 0.44) for men and Rs 15 (US$ 0.33) for women, which is not equal to minimum wages fixed by the government.

We work in 120 villages of small farmers and agricultural labourers, basically educating them about the Rights and organizing them as unions to struggle for their socio-economic Rights enshrined in the constitution of India.

We conducted a study on the land situation in the State of Andhra Pradesh in the year 1991. The study revealed that 60% of government land which is supposed to be in the hands of poor has gone into the hands of big landlords.

Following the study, we decided to work for land appropriations in order to combat poverty. Our land reform laws advocate radical distribution of land in favour of the poor people, but in reality government officers in want of bribes assign the land only for the rich. Therefore, details of illegal land transfers are disseminated to the villagers, and wherever possible the people are motivated toward land appropriation. To take back the land from the rich and distribute it to the poor is very risky for the people involved in it. Therefore we adopt different strategies to appropriate the land.

Anantapuram complex is one of the villages identified with illegally assigned government land. The assignee is a big landlord-cum-powerful politician having influence with the bureaucracy. He has assigned the land in the name of his minor children, mentioning them as major. So it is decided to take this land by the landless.

The first step in taking the land was to organize the small farmers and agricultural labourers into a union and conduct a legal education programme on applicable land laws and on how to identify and map various lands in the Anantapuram complex. Information on the lands illegally transferred to landlords was then disseminated and a collective decision for land appropriation was taken by 60 village leaders at a union meeting. They further identified the 10 most needy families among the 40 landless ones, and also decided to assign the land, once taken, in the names of women to ensure their access and control over resources, leading to women's empowerment. Women frequently complain—with surprisingly little challenge from their menfolk—that the latter squander family resources on liquor, whereas they, the women, spend it on the children and on the family as a whole.

Filing an advance caveat with the courts to prevent a landlord injunction order, the villagers proceeded to take the land, with support from 1,000 poor Dalit farmers from nearby villages who helped as guards. In response, however, Chennaiah says, 'the landlord came along with his henchmen and women carrying deadly weapons to attack the Dalits. On seeing the numerical strength they used their women to put chili powder in the eyes of the supporters and the tractor driver. (Tractor driver will need a helmet to continue to till the land in such situations!)' The Dalits then filed a police complaint against the landlord and formed a vigilance committee to protect themselves from further attacks.

Meanwhile, the landlord, soliciting support from other landlords in the area (whose positions were also under threat), accumulated an amount of Rs 60,000 (US$ 1,333) to deal with the police and the courts. Being influential in the bureaucracy and the ruling political party, the landlord intimidated the police into not filing the case, tried to divide the Dalits on subcaste lines and attacked the Dalit village again, beating up the women and children. The police did not register the case and the bureaucracy did not cancel the original land assignment to the landlord.

In response to this quite typical sequence of events, the farmers organized mass protests in front of the police station demanding that they register the case. They also organized a mass protest in front of the revenue department to press for issuance of land titles. Relay hunger strikes were organized for six days to get the titles in the names of women. Evidence of the fraudulent birthdays recorded by the landlord for his children were collected from the government school records to show the misallocation of land to minors, and his total land holding details were similarly procured to show his true colours. Meanwhile, the labourers weeded and harvested the crop on the disputed land with the support of other villagers, and the earnings from it were reserved for further collective action. After another year of continued wrangling, the people finally received the necessary support from the police and the revenue department and titles were given in the names of the women.

Chennaiah has many such stories to tell, including some where religious leaders have been known to compete with the needs of the poor and landless. In Andhra Pradesh, he points out, temples own 320,000 acres of cultivated fertile lands, much of the income from which allegedly goes not to temple upkeep but to temple trustees, who pay only nominal amounts per acre for using the land. 'When we do not have land to feed our stomachs why do lifeless Gods own lands,' is the union's slogan. Chennaiah also recounts the case of a church minister's son (ironically also an NGO leader), who inherited from his father 600 acres of land intended for distribution among Dalit families. When he did not comply with the intended distribution, union members occupied the land, upon which the son offered a compromise—that he would give a small part of the land, but not all, to the Dalits. This was not accepted on principle, and the union filed legal charges against him.

Discussion with union leaders shows a striking sophistication of both situation analysis and the tactics needed in response. Finding themselves in a potentially weak legal position, for example, they may decide on a strategy of filing false cases against landlords. The purpose here is to weaken the landlord—fighting fire with fire, as Chennaiah says—by ensnarling them in legal action and simultaneously demonstrating the labourers' strength. Union leaders frequently meet to discuss issues, including how to learn from their mistakes. Such discussions are key to capacity-building; indeed, some leaders believe that as much as half of the time of the organizers needs to be spent on various types of training.

In the Andhra case, this became particularly evident while comparing the agricultural federation's work with that of local NGOs. Some feel that the latter exist mainly to channel foreign donor funds to visible physical construction projects, preferring economic rather than political efforts in order to avoid potential legal complications. Empowerment movements such as the Andhra federation do not deny the important potential of such projects—indeed, in the Anantapuram example they assisted with the development of food crops and a credit cooperative. But they maintain that it is the primary emphasis and sequence of activities that is critical in addressing the roots of poverty and oppression. Improved cropping and credit availability will accomplish little without a prior degree of empowerment and self-reliance.

It is no simple matter to fine-tune an appropriate sequence and balance between empowering people and creating development opportunities for improved livelihoods. To the west of Chennaiah's Chittoor district is Madakasira, a relatively isolated and particularly poor part of Anantapur district, where the Centre for Rural Studies and Development (CRSD) has been working since 1992. CRSD is led by a wife–husband team known simply as Rani and Bose. Rani absorbed from as early as age ten her family's social concerns, and Bose gained social awareness through Marxist literature. While Rani and Bose are very clear in articulating the empowerment objective and community organizing strategy of CRSD, other staff members tend to describe their work in terms of individual development activities such as watershed management, health services and schools. This perhaps reflects their insufficient confidence when operating in a larger conceptual framework, or perhaps they are simply following a natural tendency to explain their work in terms that foreign donors are accustomed to hearing. Or this description of work may be related to CRSD's preference 'to build awareness gradually rather than have a dramatic or sensational impact which can lead to a serious set back by violence and repression'.

Indeed, CRSD does use traditional development activities, such as organizing the construction of small earthworks and dams, as entry points to gain access to government officials at district and state levels and to other NGOs. Simultaneously, they gain the initial confidence of the local people. Having done so, they then begin forming groups to discuss larger impediments to employment and economic advance and to press for provision of government services and accountability. CRSD purposely includes in its constituency all lower caste and Dalit groups, considering it better strategy not to confront on the basis of narrower class or caste lines (unless necessary), but to gain the cooperation of as broad a spectrum of people as possible in moving forward.

Seated Indian style on the floor of CRSD's simple office outside Madakasira town, staff members recount poignant experiences of working with different castes and social groups. Brahmin staff members, influenced no doubt by years of social conditioning, expressed initial hesitations in eating with Dalits, but they 'got over it' and now tend to be seen as role models for doing so. Dalit staff members, by the same token, were sometimes not allowed to enter upper caste homes. When required to spend nights in distant villages, they were sometimes forced to sleep outside—degrading treatment, particularly given their motivation to help in the localities. Eventually, as staff members became better known through longer exposure in the localities, they were usually accepted—itself a sign of success and a contribution to relieving oppression.

Madakasira, like far too many parts of India, is a drought-prone area; the rains fail every three years, on average. The poor, having no ready assets to tide them over, obviously suffer the most. In 2000, for example, the groundnut crop was essentially lost due to drought, the only saving grace being that there was a good tamarind crop. As elsewhere, the bargaining power of the poor for reasonable wage labour is non-existent unless they organize their forces. But organizing also brings the wrath of the upper castes and landowners. In one situation described by Madakasira organizers, Dalit labourers were threatened with sticks and simply not hired for labour; they were forced to seek work in Bangalore, the nearest large city, still relatively distant. The problem, of course, is that in areas with surplus labour (which describes much of India and many other countries), landlords have no problem finding docile replacement labour. The only recourse for the poor is to come together and refuse to work *en masse*. The risks are high, of course, and the group must have sufficient strength and confidence to dare to rock the boat.

Women tend to suffer the most, carrying the burden of low social status within the caste system along with their gender disadvantage. When CRSD began organizing village meetings with women,

we found that women were reluctant to come together; they were shy, suspicious, and generally wondered what anyone would want with them. The men would constitute 70% in a women's meeting. They would literally ask the women to 'shut up', calling them fools and good for nothing. The women always were accompanied by their husbands to the government offices, and they stood outside the office, or behind their men, while they negotiated matters relating to their wives. Women never had a space of their own where they could collectively analyse their situations and find solutions to their problems.

In response to the situation, CRSD used savings and health work as entry points into the villages. 'Through regular savings meetings, we were able to raise other issues. The men were gradually weaned out from the women's meetings. This took nearly 6 months to 1 year.'

In one village of Madakasira, the local women felt sufficiently emboldened to complain to the authorities about a schoolteacher who did not come to work. In this case, they actually succeeded in getting him transferred, but the men of the village complained that they had been bypassed in the process. Interestingly, however, the men then came to agree that women are more effective in pressing such causes. Their reasons are telling—first, women more readily join forces than do men, and second, they are not asked for bribes to the extent that men are.

CRSD illustrates the earlier noted advantages of like-minded groups sharing experiences with and supporting one another. They have significantly benefited from the nurturing role of Asmita, a women's support organization based in the Andhra Pradesh capital of Hyderabad, whose primary role is to promote socio-economic transformation by reducing gender inequalities. Asmita aims 'to help women be equal partners in the creation of a just society', and also to 'make gender an overall socio/political issue, to make people more sensitive about gender and see the development process with a gender perspective'. Started by committed feminists, Asmita took on the role of sharing experiences in the women's movement through networking, conferences, training at various levels, sponsorship of rallies, preparing audio-visual materials and publications, and providing 'a gender perspective into the whole political discourse... something absolutely essential in all issues'.

CRSD credits Asmita with helping to give 'a radical turn to CRSD work'. Sensitizing NGO leaders and staff, district writers and university students on gender issues, Asmita has also provided CRSD with inputs in training and in organizing rallies. It has conducted training for CRSD team members and grassroots women on issues such as the situation of the girl child, violence, health and panchayat raj (village government). Three CRSD-organized rallies 'have reached out to almost 10,000 women' and served as 'a kind of starting point, helpful in reaching out to masses in a short span of time. Asmita comprised the resource team which focused on broader issues in these rallies. This has been followed up with intense trainings' connected with the issues raised.

The ability of CRSD and others to draw on expertise and common solidarity from outside their local districts has proven highly important in the development of empowerment movements. As encountered in the Maharashtra and Gujarat examples recounted earlier, this type of 'family' approach allows newer groups to learn from the experiences of their predecessors and to build overall capacity with widening ripple effects. It helps local organizations combat the sense of isolation that often exists, particularly in remote rural areas, and conveys both professional and moral support and a feeling that others care. For urban-based organizations, in this case Asmita, the relationship fosters a flow of information on rural conditions, which is critical for its advocacy work in the state capital. The relationship is not only mutually supportive, therefore, but mutually empowering.

5

Power of Knowledge, Power of the Purse

Clustered at one end of a room in a house in forestland Vijayanagar, some two dozen tribal women from the surrounding areas have been expectantly waiting for the visitors from Ahmedabad—two hot, dusty hours away by road. Whereas two years ago these same women had been silent and lacking in confidence, on this day they are all abuzz, ready to volunteer information and answer questions about their lives and aspirations. None of them, it turns out, has attended school for even a minimal three years, yet every single one of them now has either her own children or her grandchildren in school. While this certainly represents progress, even more striking is the saga of their improved livelihoods.

In Gujarat, more than 100,000 tribal women are said to work as *tendu* leaf pickers in the months of April and May each year. During the leaf picking season, they get up early in the mornings and go to the forests, usually quite a long distance away. There they climb up the *tendu* trees to pluck the leaves (used to roll *bidis*—popular Indian cigarettes). It takes more than eight hours to pluck about five thousand leaves, and there is always the possibility of falling off a tree by accident and sustaining injuries. The women then bring the leaves home to arrange them in 100 bundles of 50 leaves each; they must count out each leaf, which requires considerable time.

Having arranged the leaves in bundles, the women then take them in a basket or in a piece of cloth to the collection centre, again quite a distance to walk, and deposit the leaves there. The collection rate for the 1998 season was Rs 35 (US$ 0.78) for 100 bundles.

Seeing the hardship involved for minimal remuneration, an organization called DISHA decided to help the women achieve more just prices. They reported,

> ...we started the process by keeping in mind the logistics of the time schedule, because normally the ministry of forest and environment, along with the Gujarat forest development corporation, appoints a price fixing committee in the month of December, and by the end of it the collection price for the season is fixed up, and then these prices are advertised in newspapers and tenders are floated for the parties to bid.
>
> We started well in advance in November 1998 and submitted memoranda of demand that the collection prices be raised to Rs 45 (US$ 1) for one hundred bundles. The memoranda were submitted by all the [producer] groups. Simultaneously we got an article published in newspapers with statistical calculations supporting our argument for raising the collection prices; [it appeared] every week in different newspapers, English as well Gujarati. *The Sandesh*, a Gujarati daily, carried the news on its front page, titled 'Exploitation of Tribal Women for Prosperity of Traders'. This was published by all editions on the same day in Ahmedabad, Baroda, Rajkot, and Surat city, and it created ripples in the ministry and FDC [forest development corporation].

The Gujarat state forest development corporation's price fixing committee increased the collection rate to Rs 37.50, a net increment of Rs 2.50 per hundred bundles—not the full amount requested, but nevertheless a 7 per cent increase that benefited some 100,000 tribal women to the tune of Rs 6.25 million in additional income.

DISHA, which stands for Developing Initiatives for Social and Human Action, was founded by M.D. Mistry, a former union leader (along with SEWA's Ela Bhatt) who also worked for several years on the staff of Oxfam, a highly regarded relief and development NGO. DISHA's efforts go well beyond those of most NGOs. It describes itself as 'a mass-based and membership-based organization working towards improvement of economic and social conditions of marginalized classes like landless people, labourers, tribals, dalits, women, etc. through their empowerment in order to influence control and use of natural and economic resources'. Beyond fostering village level groups, trade unions, issue-based groups, cooperatives and women's groups—efforts not dissimilar to those of other groups cited here—DISHA's most unique contribution stems from its work in budget analysis and advocacy.

Mistry is the first to admit that there was no planned approach to DISHA's development. Its activities 'grew organically as it went on realizing the need to do something during the course of work'. In common with other movement leaders, he and his colleagues continually sought the *source* of the constraints to improved living situations for the poor. For example, they realized that agricultural labourers needed but did not have identity cards in order to avail of government welfare benefits. DISHA worked with the labourers to ensure that the government issued them identity cards, which constituted a major breakthrough for the labourers. It allowed them to take advantage of a number of government programmes, releasing them from the previously constant necessity of having to pay bribes to demonstrate their identity and thus eligibility for the programmes.

Similarly, DISHA observed that workers whose families had been cultivating forestland for generations often lacked official authorization and were thus subject to harassment and fines. In 1996, under the banner of a DISHA-inspired union,

> over 2,000 farmers from all over the tribal belt gathered in the state capital. The press highlighted the forest land cultivators' issue which compelled the Forest Minister to call the delegation for discussion, and finally he agreed to implement the earlier resolution of the government to provide land titles to forest-land cultivators numbering 67,000.

Between the financial benefits from higher *tendu* leaf prices and the security and welfare benefits from land titles and identity cards, the tribal people made significant gains.

DISHA's focus on improving financial benefits for the poor through improved government policies and implementation of established laws led to further thinking on the issue. Mistry writes,

It was an after-thought in the early 90s that DISHA got involved in budget analysis. DISHA believes that in order to improve the economic and social condition of the poor, *merely organising* them is not sufficient. The leadership of the poor also needs to educate itself in the science of economics. It needs to learn and understand how the economic and financial resources of the state are distributed and spent. These resources are controlled or manipulated through the instrument of the budget.

While working with the tribals and other labourers [DISHA] felt the need of looking into the 'spending' in the tribal areas by the government. This led to looking into the entire budget. And to understand the budget we had to understand the technical terms used in the budget documents. We studied budget manuals, reports of finance commissions, the Indian accounting system, and a number of other areas.

We got acquainted with the 'figures' and designed the classification of budget data according to the government accounting system. Getting familiar with the budget documents and co-relating them with the economic and social conditions of vulnerable groups was difficult in the beginning. But once we got familiar, we began to look at all our issues and problems in the new financial perspective too. Understanding the budget changed our vision and perspective completely. And it is in this perspective that we began to see how the budget can be a very accurate tool to measure any state government's commitment to social development, or to the economic, social, and cultural rights.

Mistry notes, for example, that 'when reading carefully through the budget we find lakhs [hundreds of thousands] of rupees that are just miscalculated and missing from the budget'. DISHA then looked at the constitutional and legal provisions for tribal people in the state to discover what the government should be allocating for their needs.

We found what we were asking from the state, be it minimum wages, land, etc., was merely a peanut as compared to the money the state was spending for other purposes. Every department of the state should be spending on the tribal areas, so we must look at all the budgets of all the departments to see what they should be giving tribals. To our surprise, the tribal areas got as little as 1–2% of the money in the budgets [subsequently increased to just over 4 per cent] when their fair share, based on proportion of population, should be at least 15%. We looked at how the money was being spent instead of on tribals and created a booklet on the situation. We sent the booklet out to the parliament, bureaucracy, and media. This created a huge stir! Because the facts were hard, the government could not deny their bad treatment of the tribals. Tribals were able to organize around this information and win battles.

The government always says it has no money to do work for tribals, but now we have proof that the money is there. This has helped to win court cases and get provisions for the tribals. The group is able to demand employment creation in the villages, and the government has complied. The lesson to be learned is that the state finances put money in the hands of the people who already have it, and don't help out the tribals or dalits. The pattern of allocation is completely in favor of the powerful. Budget analysis gives groups a tool to use against any opponent—the government, landlords, etc. Knowing the finance will allow you to tell the government they do have the money to implement the laws favoring tribals. Budget analysis also shows that the service sector constitutes much of the revenue the state receives. The poor also contribute a lot to the revenue, through sales and other indirect taxes which constitute over 50% of Gujarat state tax revenues, but do not receive the benefits of the budget.

To enable village, block and district level leaders to better press their claims to government resources, DISHA conducts workshops for individuals from these local levels. Their objectives are to ensure an understanding of the importance of the budget, of budgetary procedures and functioning, of how to perceive a problem and express an appropriate solution in budgetary terms and how to advocate for such solutions with the people's full participation.

A DISHA workshop report illuminates the difficulties participants face in preparing their village budgets. One *sarpanch* (head of the *panchayat*—village governing body) from Mahudi village of Dahod district pointed out,

we would like to introduce drip irrigation for farming in villages of border areas. But the forest department is not giving us permission. Therefore we approached to higher government authorities, but nobody is ... paying ... attention to our grievances. This has hampered our development.

Similarly, a former woman *sarpanch* of Fatehpura village in Sabar-kantha district said, 'When we ladies are selected as sarpanch of village we face a lot of problems. Such as the other members and colleagues do not co-operate in the administration, saying that women do not understand the technicalities of administration.' She then raised her voice and emphasized that 'we [women] do govern and administer the household expenditure. We also are equally capable to administer and govern the administrative tech-nicalities of budget preparation.'

On the positive side, another *sarpanch* discussed methods of increasing available income by imposing taxes on village shops and on the products of local mines, while another said, 'I utilized the MLAs [legislators] fund, district development fund and other aids to solve the problem of my village'. He then offered examples of how he had done so. A DISHA leader stressed the advantages of going to political leaders for support, especially at election time when campaign promises can be followed up on to make sure they are reflected in budget documents.

Whatever the timing, the importance of local budget analysis is as clear as that of state and national level analyses. This point is stressed in the admonition of a sub-district leader who noted in a DISHA workshop that only 1.42 per cent of expenditures in his area were devoted to social welfare, with the result that very few people benefited from them. He said,

> If the beneficiaries are to be increased, and to increase the operational effectiveness of social welfare, the *sarpanches*/representatives have to mark their needs and wants in the budget books when they are prepared. So it means that if the social upliftment is to be done then one needs to understand and interpret budget properly.

How important is budget analysis? Although cost–benefit analysis is not normally associated with the activities of either development NGOs or empowerment movements, DISHA has attempted to suggest some impacts of such an exercise and has emerged with striking insights. A specific case—simplistic, perhaps, but highly plausible—follows by way of example:

In the period 1996–98, at DISHA members' urging, the state government distributed 124,000 acres of land to forestland culti-vators. If one assumes that 100,000 of those acres are cultivated every year at a net income rate of Rs 1,000 (US$ 22.22) each, the total net income from this forestland over two years would be Rs 200 million (US$ 4.4 million). In addition, DISHA calculates a saving of Rs 10.2 million (US$ 226,667) in fines which the tribals would no longer be obliged to pay. If one adds in the value of the some 25,000 acres of land for which 22,000 tribal farmers received cultivation entitlement letters and land titles, at the normal purchase price of Rs 10,000 (US$ 222) per acre, the total value of the land freely transferred from the state government to the tribals amounts to Rs 250 million (US$ 5.55 million). One should further include the increase by Rs 5 per 100 bundles for *tendu* leaf pickers during 1996–98 (from Rs 30 to Rs 35, before they received the Rs 2.5 increase in 1998). The value of the increase for the women leaf pickers comes to Rs 20 million (US$ 444,444) over two years. Finally, 170 labourers were made permanent employees of the forest department as a result of the Forest Labourers' Union's fighting on their behalf. In addition to the regular minimum income of at least Rs 42,000 assured for every worker (Rs 7.1 million, or US$ 157,778, for all the workers), a court order granted Rs 9 million (US$ 200,000) in arrears.

Added together, the result is a total benefit of Rs 496.3 million (US$ 11.03 million). DISHA's programme spending during the two years was approximately Rs 6.77 million (US$ 150,444) and its total spending, including amounts spent on supportive activities such as budget analyses and capital expenditure, was approximately Rs 12.17 million (US$ 282,222). The net result calculated on the basis of programme spending is a cost–benefit ratio of 1:73. With all expenses accounted for, every 1 rupee spent by DISHA brought in 41 rupees in return. And this does not begin to factor in continuing, *future* benefits.

According to a DISHA report,

> These are the economic benefits achieved but we find it difficult to calculate the cost of the other two policy decisions, which are not included in the cost benefit ratio:
>
> (A) The government announced that all the forest land will now be in the joint names of the men and women. Thus for the first time women would be the joint asset-holders.
>
> (B) With our efforts the state government took another policy decision [noted earlier] to issue identity cards to 36 lakh (3.6 million)

agricultural labourers. The identity cards relieve the agricultural labourers from the hassles and harassment of the lower
level revenue and other functionaries of the state government
while claiming the benefits of government programmes. The
Gujarat government would be the first government in India to
issue such cards.

Perhaps most important, as Mistry adds, is the increasing
recognition at both state and national levels that, first, notwithstanding five decades of government five-year plans and well
meaning policies, poverty and oppression continue to a shocking
degree; second, the poor's claims to rights as full citizens of India,
particularly to the right to human dignity, are legitimate; and third,
government budgets must focus on visibly changing the quality
of life of this poorest sector of society.

'How does one calculate the monetary benefits against the efforts
put in?' Mistry asks. 'The answer would be best left to the reader.'

Such dramatic success may seem unbelievable or due to factors
and influences beyond the efforts of DISHA alone. Yet there is no
doubting the effectiveness of DISHA's budget efforts.
DISHA reports,

> Like common people, most social action groups, journalists, and
> even the academics, who don't have the discipline of public finance,
> and especially budget-analysis, avoid taking interest in the budget,
> which is the most comprehensive annual financial statement of the
> government. Since financial statements are expressed in the figures,
> and figures generally make people uncomfortable, they simply put
> the budget documents or company balance sheets aside and are
> forced to accept or rather surrender to the expert's word at its face
> value.

DISHA emphasizes the importance of the budget process as, on
the one hand, it articulates the financial position of the state, indi-
cating intended expenditures as well as receipts through taxes,
loans, advances, etc.; and, on the other hand, it declares the government's plans for generating employment—either directly in

government bodies or by measures to augment the working of private companies and entrepreneurs, and through providing relief to the poor, the aged, women and other vulnerable sections of the society through social sector spending. The budget is thus the publicly expressed intention of the government to carry out particular activities—a commitment to undertaking certain initiatives during a financial year.

Without denigrating the work of other groups, DISHA notes that,

> Most of the social action groups, NGOs, or membership-based organisations mainly concentrate their activity around the legal system and the laws. They are either engaged in enforcement or implementation of the law, or seeking justice in the courts through law. There is hardly any membership-based organisation which relates its activities with the financial management of the state, or worries about its constituency's share in the state's financial cake.

DISHA's budget analysis has thus attracted particular attention among other movement leaders and has begun to serve as an example to empowerment groups elsewhere in India and beyond. The Ford Foundation, for example, has begun to sponsor national workshops on the subject, which have included a number of international representatives.

Budget analysis complements in important and persuasive ways the efforts of struggle movements. If organizing the poor and strengthening their advocacy capacities is the first prerequisite for combating oppression, and if traditional development approaches to improve livelihoods and social services constitute a subsidiary tool to that end, budget analysis has now been shown to be a valued third prong creating additional impetus to propel movements forward.

6

Variations on the Theme

Empowerment movements evolve in a variety of ways and take on multiple forms, as the previous chapters have shown. The Pandits began with pigs and goats in an attempt to increase the incomes of poor villagers until they discovered that the more fundamental problem to be solved was that of bonded labour. Martin Macwan, outraged by the murderous oppression of fellow Dalits by caste Hindus, initiated his movement with the single-minded objective of changing social power relationships, recognizing later that development activities were also needed in order to consolidate the livelihoods of the newly enfranchised. Ela Bhatt arrived at her vision of empowerment through a combination of organizing and development initiatives, with the understanding that economic wherewithal and political voice are inseparable parts of self-reliant development. M.D. Mistry's unique contribution has been to invoke the power of budget analysis as a tool for advocacy in favour of the rights of the oppressed.

Other groups and leaders have taken their commitments into different directions, two examples of which are worth examining here—one in the north Indian state of Rajasthan and the other in Gujarat. In another variation on the theme, responses to the tragic earthquake in Gujarat in January 2001 demonstrate the relevance and importance of an empowerment approach in emergency relief situations.

Social worker Sharad Joshi had joined relief operations in Rajasthan in the wake of devastating floods in 1982, which gutted and eroded entire crop fields and buried whole villages under sand dunes that stood fifteen feet high. The extent of soil erosion is said to have been so bad that entire wells, previously underground, stood like tall chimneys sticking out of the sand. Sharad had been determined to mobilize a long-term rehabilitation response to strengthen the local community. Land reclamation, provision of drinking water (all the more critical in light of subsequent droughts) and overall natural resource management became a major focus of his new organization, the Centre for Community Economics and Development Consultants (CECOEDECON). CECOEDECON also conducted a variety of education and income-generation projects, managing to obtain financial support from a large number of Indian government and foreign donor sources. In fact, CECOEDECON soon became a more-or-less typical development organization.

New insights were developed in the early 1990s when Sharad and one of his deputies attended courses at the Advocacy Training Institute in Washington, DC. (Other Indian movement leaders have attended the same course.) However, rather than attempting to convert CECOEDECON itself into an empowerment-oriented advocacy organization, its leaders decided to give advocacy support to several small local groups in Rajasthan with which CECOEDECON was affiliated in a network relationship. The Dedwana salt campaign was among the first of these.

The problem in Dedwana was that salt was produced by labourers who were not allowed to sell their produce on the open market. Rather, they had to sell it at the government rate of only Rs 9.30 per quintal (1997 rate), whereas on the open market salt fetched Rs 21 to Rs 28 per quintal. Furthermore, as described in a CECOEDECON report,

> The status of the producers has never been clearly defined. They are considered both labourers and manufacturers simultaneously, and their circumstances combine the worst of both worlds. For instance, because they are considered labourers, they are not allowed to sell their salt on the open market. However, because they are considered manufacturers, they are also not given minimum wage for their work. An additional and equally serious problem is that

the labourers do not get their payment on time, if at all. For every quintal of salt produced, 35 paise have been deducted from their pay for water, medical treatment, and a rest house; however no actual facilities have been provided.

In the 1980s, prior to CECOEDECON's involvement, efforts had been made to ensure that the salt workers receive either minimum wage or leasing rights to the salt pans. At that time, the state's High Court had required payment of minimum wage and, furthermore, that women, even if their names were not recorded, should be assumed to be doing the same job and should be equally paid. The judgment had been in English, however, and since the workers had not understood the proceedings, they had been misled into believing that they had actually lost the case.

The Dedwana salt workers' struggle became increasingly public in the 1990s when a local journalist wrote about their plight in regional and later in statewide Hindi language newspapers. It was at this point, in 1996, that CECOEDECON came into the picture. Upon participating in a workshop organized by CECOEDECON after its leaders had attended the course at the Advocacy Institute, the journalist was encouraged to set up an NGO to support the salt struggle. CECOEDECON then offered support to the NGO, Sukshma Vigyan Samiti, through training and funding for the salt workers' cause.

Sukshma Vigyan Samiti conducted an in-depth survey and collected extensive material, including a list of the current leasers of the salt land, legal and other actions taken on salt issues in the past and data on salt producers and their living conditions in 34 villages. They then lobbied for a solution to the salt workers' problems. They organized and provided legal aid for the producers, tried to obtain past payments due to them and organized them to lobby for required facilities (water, treatment facilities and housing) and for the right to sell salt on the open market.

Ignoring, for whatever reasons, the earlier court judgment requiring payment of minimum wage, they pressured the government into issuing a notification of privatization that would give leasing rights to the producers and, therefore, allow them to sell their salt on the open market. The problem was that leasing rights in Dedwana demanded very heavy royalties on the land—between Rs 2,900–6,000 per pan per annum, which was one hundred times higher than the lease rate on salt pans in other areas of Rajasthan. The consequence of such heavy royalties was that only the rich and powerful had the capacity to acquire the salt pans for production, which would leave the salt producers in their previous unacceptable condition. A case against these royalties was then brought before the High Court of Rajasthan.

The CECOEDECON report concludes with an analysis of the impact of these actions.

> The salt producers ... organised and participated in sit-ins and non-violent agitations, and the plight of the salt producers was also picked up by local media (newspapers in particular). Out of the local community, NGO, and union efforts, the back-payments due to 1049 out of the 1167 producers were obtained. Salt production has been privatised, which means they are allowed to sell salt in the open market for the next 10 years (i.e. until 2008).

More recently, the royalty rates have reportedly been reduced to a more acceptable level.

Evaluating the local group's efforts, CECOEDECON listed certain 'opportunities for improvement', noting that

- the minimum wage issue was never pursued
- the partner NGO is already somewhat expert in advocacy, and the training provided by CECOEDECON is too general (needs to be more specialised)[outside observers would consider this an understatement, noting that the training was definitely not sufficiently strategic or specific to the local context]
- the salt campaign could be a good demonstration model for other campaigns, but currently documentation is weak, so there is little written material that can be provided to other campaigns
- in spite of all the efforts CECOEDECON and Sukshma Vigyan Samiti have made, the government reaction remains unpredictable (e.g. the high royalties levied on the land)
- the ten year limit on the right to sell salt on the open market offers no long term solution for the salt producers

Outside observers would add that CECOEDECON placed excessive effort on monitoring and controlling the local groups in an overly 'big brother' style at the expense of fostering local decision-making and independence. They also note that a large share of resources intended to support the local groups went to CECOEDECON itself.

What differentiates CECOEDECON from the groups previously discussed is partly the very notion of advocacy as *one* of the major strategies rather than as the *overriding* one—and even then, more for the groups affiliated to it than for CECOEDECON itself. While its staggering array of development projects has earned it the support of many, largely European, funders, CECOEDECON is clearly not an empowerment movement. The organization's reaction upon discovering cases of bonded labour, for example, has been to work around the problem rather than tackle it head-on; 'we can't take on every issue,' has been their response. The reasons for this lack of action priority seem to include the leadership's aversion to risk-taking, resistance among long-time staff with traditional outlooks, and a lack of interest on the part of most funders to support such activities (an issue discussed in Chapter Eight). This, then, is where CECOEDECON differs from the other groups described in this volume; although it tackles some issues relating to human rights, it is not at heart a rights-based organization.

Should all of CECOEDECON's resources be directed toward advocacy and empowerment activities, or is there utility and virtue in pursuing traditional development projects—such as projects in soil and water conservation, health clinics and micro-credit for women's enterprises? The organization's self-assessment shows commendable results from many of these projects in terms of increased agricultural production, greater availability of health services and increased income for women. These are no small accomplishments. The question, as always, is whether the power of the poor has simultaneously been built up to the extent that they can lobby for their own just needs on a self-sustaining basis in the future.

In Ahmedabad, Gujarat, Dr Hanif Lakdawala took quite a different tack. As a physician, he initially saw the need for healthcare for poor urban slum dwellers and he started a clinic for them under the institutional name of Sanchetana. Philosophizing on his original motivation, Hanif wrote,

The genesis of Sanchetana can be traced to my subjective need and appraisal of the objective reality. Subjective need was to create a niche to self-actualize, to fulfill my metaneeds. Objective reality was that the world was a little too unjust, a little too unequal, a little too exploitative. It could be, if not transformed completely, changed to a little better, a little more livable world. The existential suffering of the lonely crowd could be ameliorated. For urban slum dwellers, abundant health services are available in forms of government and private hospitals and dispensaries, which paradoxically puts them in a disadvantaged position. Government hospitals and dispensaries are irrelevant to some extent because of their lack of understanding of real health problems of poor people and so are not equipped to deal with them effectively. Moreover, most of the poor people find these services repulsive because of the inhuman treatment meted out to them. On the other hand, private health services are inhumanly extortionist in nature. Thus, to demystify medicine for the common people, [I] channelized [my] efforts in the areas of health and education. It was only a starting point. The main objective was to empower the poor and to build their capacity to stand collectively against exploitation and discrimination. The health care system was only one of the paradigms of the exploitative systems of society.

With the benefit of psychiatric training, Hanif was able to articulate, in addition to the socio-political dimension, the psychological dimension of the problem, observing that 'the community [of urban slum dwellers] held a negative, demeaning view of itself due to their near-survival, traumatic life, which leads to a notion of "accommodation", where people perceive no possibility of redemption'. Health, like the Pandits' pigs and goats, thus became the entry point to larger concerns over the poor's low buying capacity, low status of women, low literacy and inadequate water and sanitation, among others. By responding to such an obvious and widely felt community need as that for improved health services, Sanchetana staff soon built up the credibility needed for engaging in other activities, including income-generating efforts and skills training, as well as the formation of men's and women's groups and initiatives aimed at promoting basic rights and communal harmony.

Given the significant numbers of Muslims in Ahmedabad, this last effort presented particular challenges, which became particularly dramatic in the wake of devastating communal riots in 1992. Shocked by the riots, and his fellow Muslims' fear of the majority Hindus, Hanif quickly perceived communal relations as a further, damaging challenge to community health. Spurred by the tense situation, he founded the Institute for Initiative in Education (IFIE). The new organization was to be dedicated to promoting dialogue among educated Indian Muslims, identifying Muslims' problems, strengthening the influence of moderates over extremists and evolving comprehensive strategies to improve the situation. The focus would be on the entire nation, not only on the local communities with which Sanchetana had been working. Further, IFIE would foster a process of introspection and dialogue among Indian Muslims and other communities, to evolve comprehensive strategies to combat the evil of communalism, beyond improving the status of Muslims alone. Consultations were held and committees involving hundreds of individuals were formed along these lines. As an essentially middle class undertaking, it clearly constituted a different approach than that of the other movements cited here. Gradually, though, the consultations did spread out to include poorer, less educated people and communities, as the middle class groups were increasingly urged to work with them.

While Sanchetana's health and other community activities continued, and still continue, the development of a new focus on Muslim and communal issues could hardly have been predicted at the outset. The striking point here is that however important health is to well-being, underlying realities—even if they are as different in nature from healthcare as religious discrimination—must be tackled if the poor are to have any chance for meaningful, self-sustaining development. Furthermore, social realities may sometimes suggest a modified approach—in this case, working with people whose commonality of religion (Islam) may be seen as more important, at least as a first step, than any class differences among them. Most NGOs working on health might determine that such a new direction of activity is best left to others, that their mission is to stick to healthcare, or whatever applies in individual cases. What appears to be unique about Hanif and the other leaders described in this volume is their commitment to pursuing at all costs the *fundamental* problems, whether it be that of bonded labour, generalized caste oppression, discrimination against women or communal violence.

One of the factors contributing to India's oppressive poverty is the subcontinent's susceptibility to disasters—not only man-made, such as the communal violence confronted by Hanif Lakdawala and his colleagues, but also natural disasters, such as the floods encountered by Sharad Joshi early in his career, not to mention chronic droughts and periodic earthquakes.

On January 26, 2001, as India was celebrating Republic Day with parades and festivities across the nation, a massive earthquake struck the state of Gujarat, home to several of the organizations whose work is described in this volume. Measuring 7.9 on the Richter scale, it caused major damage in the Kutch region, bordering Pakistan, as well as in adjoining districts and the city of Ahmedabad. Kutch is particularly prone to natural calamities, having suffered two severe cyclones in the late 1990s and droughts of increasing intensity, including one ongoing at the time of the earthquake. Dry under the best of conditions, its agricultural economy is poor, capable of producing only one crop a year in most parts of the district; animal husbandry, once a significant income-earner for some, has declined in recent years. Renowned for superior handicrafts—especially block printing, tie-dye and mirror work—the area had recently overcome some of its previous marketing obstacles through the important contributions of NGOs such as SEWA.

While the most serious loss of life, out of the 20,000 estimated deaths (with some estimates citing substantially higher figures), occurred in urban areas among residents of tall buildings that collapsed and buried them, the suffering in rural areas was at least as overwhelming. Visitors to a village in Surendranagar district, where many houses had toppled, were received by a SEWA member in the courtyard of her house where she and her family were living under a blue plastic sheet. She said that until four years ago when she had joined SEWA, she had been very poor and barred by caste custom from leaving the shack she called home. Joining SEWA's savings and credit group, which she now headed, had allowed her to get out of the clutches of the moneylender and obtain a loan with which she had built a new and better house. She had just made the last repayment on the loan for the house the previous month. There it lay in ruins as she wept.

In addition to losing their homes, rural people often lost food and seed stocks, along with their agricultural tools because of the normal practice of storing the harvest in the farmer's house, along with the seeds for the following year's sowing. The people, therefore, clearly needed not only immediate relief in the form of blankets and tarpaulins to shelter them from the elements, but also means of assuring their future livelihoods and earning power. The transition from relief to rehabilitation is a critical part of disaster planning and implementation.

Surendranagar's women, at least, were in a slightly better situation because of SEWA's forward thinking. First, they were members of a SEWA social security (insurance) scheme that could come to at least partial aid in such a situation (nothing short of a massive, presumably government-supported scheme could have coped with the circumstances of the 2001 earthquake). Second, the women had benefited from a training programme that had taught them the skills necessary to repair the damaged village water tank. Access to water being a serious problem, and with no outside aid available in time, they took it upon themselves to make the necessary repairs and restore water supply for their families' use. The women also went door-to-door to check on the survival and well-being of community members, surveying and then communicating their most urgent needs to those in a position to help.

Lack of understanding of local needs is a critical problem in emergency relief efforts. All too often, albeit with the best of intentions, donors pour in massive amounts of useless, or at least not priority, items, which tend to clutter nearby airports and warehouses. Of what use is powdered milk if there is no potable water with which to mix it? Of what use are second-hand western shoes or modish clothes when people are shivering in the night-time desert cold for lack of blankets or scorching in the daytime sun for lack of simple tarpaulin or tent shelters? Through Navsarjan and related groups in Gujarat, appeals were broadcast on the Internet to *not* send certain useless items, but to send, instead, those items most direly needed or money with which to buy them—such as tarpaulins for shelter.

Although one hesitates to criticize well-meaning international agencies, they do sometimes create problems for local groups. While a handful work through on-site NGOs to ensure maximum relevance of their inputs, others are less sensitive or, worse, more opportunistic in seeking to enrich their own coffers or gain favourable publicity. One major international NGO came to Gujarat, opened its own office and began hiring staff at multiple times the local salary standards, bypassing and thus effectively competing for personnel with the local organizations. At least one women's group from a foreign embassy was cited as having raised major resources for expensive mobile vans to be used as classrooms, when the primary need was for funding teachers and rehabilitation organizers who could just as easily have taught under trees or tarpaulins during the immediate post-emergency period. A top-down tradition infects disaster relief as much as it does development activities, in both cases tending to disenfranchise the poor or, at best, result in misguided resource allocations.

In the wake of Gujarat's earthquake, reports circulated that those most in need tended to be least cared for, and even discriminated against. One newspaper reported that in one of the villages where the tremors had reduced the main street to rubble, burying a procession of small girls, villagers had worked together for hours to collect and cremate more than 400 dead bodies. The leaders of the poorest groups contended that when the first of the aid trucks appeared the next day, members of the dominant castes diverted them towards their own people. 'For the first three days we had nothing to eat,' a Dalit villager complained. 'They told the trucks to avoid us and said we were disease-ridden.' The Jains, it turned out, had started a relief kitchen, but only the upper castes were encouraged to eat there.

The Dalit Solidarity Network cited other such examples and claimed that India's caste system is so pervasive that it affected much of the aid distribution in the aftermath of the earthquake. They dreamed of rebuilding destroyed villages in a way that banished segregation along caste lines. The immediate reality was hardly promising, however, as reports circulated of orphans being identified by their faces and features and placed only with families of their 'own supposed caste group'—a practice that one military commandant justified on the grounds that 'forcing people to live with different communities would not be the right thing to do.

There might be a law and order problem. After all, these people have lived apart for centuries'. In a situation where relief is often given through political party or caste group affiliation, or more concentrated in urban areas, Navsarjan and its partner NGOs monitored on an ongoing basis the provision of support to the most marginalized people and advocated on their behalf. They also conducted surveys of rehabilitation needs for these groups, complementing the work of the Ahmedabad-based Disaster Mitigation Institute, which had for some years been pressing the government and others to plan ahead for just such contingencies.

The necessity of local input is especially critical in the post-disaster rehabilitation stage. The rehabilitation process must be owned by the affected population if it is to be effective, not only in restoring and hopefully improving their livelihoods, but preferably also in redressing past injustices in the society. Local involvement is necessary on a psychological level too, in helping to ensure a level of dignity after the disaster. As stated in a SEWA document,

> Any natural disaster of these dimensions leaves some of the affected people in a state of shock and apathy; it is therefore imperative to employ them in useful activities, so that the apathy period can be minimized... [T]his 'opportunity' could be availed of to address other long-term problems, such as the drought-proofing envisaged by the State Government, and any other common assets which could then 'belong' to the new world these people will live in.

The empowerment approach thus calls for an understanding of the role of the disempowered in taking charge of their own destiny, and for providing training inputs for analysis and methodologies for implementation of rehabilitation programmes.

In the case of the Gujarat earthquake, according to the women of SEWA, 'the process should aim at the economic development of Kutch itself, and should not succumb to the designs of "do-gooders" with vested interests, which shall benefit areas other than Kutch in their implementation. Equally, due weightage should be given to the finer points of traditional systems.' With respect to housing, therefore,

> under no circumstances should the construction be contracted out, as this would reduce the 'ownership' factor, create new dependencies

on technology providers and do nothing for the local economy... The process would be strongly enhanced by organizing the affected people to go through the rubble of their houses for reusable materials and to recover such belongings as they can. The first reports coming in indicate that the affected people are inclined to rebuild their houses themselves, with a little help in terms of cement, roofing sheets, small interest free loans, etc. This process should be strongly encouraged.

Furthermore, they go on to say,

in cases where the house collapse has resulted in loss of stored food grains, seeds and agricultural implements, one would need to look at food security up to the next harvest. The rejuvenation of traditional water collection and harvesting structures, and the introduction of viable and sustainable technologies for water availability, as a means of drought proofing should be well planned. The technologies and end-products have to be 'owned' by the affected population... The same rule of involvement of the local population can apply equally to the other basic infrastructural requirement—schools, health posts, Primary Health Centres (PHCs), etc.

While Gujarat's water supply, power and communications facilities seemed to be limping back to normal relatively quickly, schooling and health delivery systems and, even more so, social welfare services, appeared to be lower on the priority list.

The issues around disaster response are thus not, in the end, very different from those surrounding the daily disaster of poverty and oppression faced by so many of India's, and the world's, people. They are simply variations on the theme. In all cases, the poor suffer the most. The only long-term solution is to achieve a level of empowerment where they can take control of their own lives, make their own decisions and ensure not only sustainable livelihoods for themselves but a more just society for all.

7

Lessons Learned

The foregoing case stories have provided a few examples of how some groups in India support the oppressed in their quest for better lives through empowerment. They reflect the belief that the more traditional development project approach, so common in the annals of government and foreign aid circles, cannot succeed in achieving comprehensive or long-lasting change; that its focus is generally too narrow and does not address the structural impediments to poor people's ability to advance in society. Rather, they hold, collective strength of the people is the *sine qua non* for success.

This chapter brings together some of the approaches used by the movements discussed earlier, analyses based on their leaders' reflections and, implicitly, some lessons learned from their experiences.

Poverty and oppression have multiple causes and, therefore, multiple issues must be addressed to overcome them. Movement leaders agree that a holistic approach is essential. For purposes of analysis, however, and to have a clearer set of prisms through which to view the experiences, the issues are viewed, and the lessons assessed, through the following lenses in this chapter: First, by summarizing and synthesizing the efforts dealing with land, livelihoods and government accountability; and second, by reviewing the methods used for grappling with these issues—specifically, organizing, advocacy and strengthening people's and

organizations' capacities. Chapter Eight examines modes of optimal donor support and partnership.

Land

In India's still largely agrarian society, land is obviously a fundamental asset, indeed key to survival. Key, too, is the quality of the
land—the degree to which it is tillable; often, if land has been
distributed to the poor at all, it has tended to be the worst land,
which may have little or no agricultural value (or require a level
of investment unaffordable by the poor). India's land reform laws
are often observed in the breach, as also are laws relating to tenancy
rights for those who work, but do not own, the land. Land en-
croachment by the wealthy and even by local religious groups is
common. Knowledge of the law is thus a critical requirement in
poor people's ability to assert their rights. As one leader puts it,
'Law is the weapon to bring the opponent to the bargaining table
and to fight campaigns,' to which must be added the need to
thoroughly and accurately document the relevant land records
before undertaking any case, and then making one's appeal on
legal, not emotional or humanitarian grounds.

Each type of land calls for a different strategy, with every case
requiring documented proof of possession, of length of possession
and related information. In tribal areas, for example, one must
also know the applicable tribal protection laws. The fact that the
country's Atrocities Act is applicable to the taking of land can also
be useful in strengthening one's case on behalf of the poor. Beyond
knowing the law, one must know how to interpret it, since opponents (typically, rich vested interests and higher castes) will inevitably choose different interpretations. It follows, then, that one
must know the opponents, as well as actual and potential allies, to
ensure maximum strength for the struggle for rights. One can further increase one's strength by enlisting media coverage through
which allies and opponents alike can be influenced to help achieve
a satisfactory resolution.

Underlying everything, of course, is effective organizing among
the concerned people themselves. A moving example of this
occurred during a meeting of movement leaders in Maharashtra.
A few miles from the meeting site, a plot of land held sacred by

local tribals had been fenced off by abutting landowners to the obvious consternation of the local village government leaders and people. Members of the Shramjeevi Sanghatna union, supported by Vidhayak Sansad, took down the fence in a declaration that this land could not be taken from the locals. Hours after the meeting concluded, a delegation of the tribals appeared at the meeting site to report that their case had been upheld by the local authorities, and to thank the Sanghatna and Vidhayak Sansad leaders for their support. Their irrepressible triumphant smiles served as persuasive recognition of the power of organizing.

Livelihoods

While land is perhaps the major resource on which to build livelihoods, rural people without the possibility of owning land need satisfactory tenancy rights, reasonable and enforced minimum wage and/or alternative employment possibilities. The last is also critical for the rapidly increasing numbers of urban poor. An example from SEWA is illustrative: SEWA began organizing women tobacco workers in Gujarat in 1984 to help them deal with powerful landlords who were paying them only a third of the minimum wage, as well as making them dependent through exploitative moneylending practices. Health was another problem, since the workers were exposed to tobacco and pesticides and often got sick, while the introduction of mechanization caused others to lose their jobs altogether. When the landlords learned of the initial organizing meetings, they fired a few women from work on these grounds in order to intimidate them, and even made death threats against them.

In response to all this, SEWA helped organize the women into a union to rally against the landlords, insisting on the implementation of minimum wage and worker protection laws. They also started savings and credit groups for the women, to wean them of their dependence on the landlords. Media exposure helped to create awareness of the positive impacts of these activities and to gain new allies for the union. Simultaneously, SEWA worked to keep open the lines of communication with the landlords, gaining their sympathy, for example, by opening (non-controversial) child-care centres. Meanwhile, other workers were also organized, including handloom weavers, who were then linked with buyers in order to provide women another source of income and reduce their dependency as well.

As expressed by SEWA's leaders, the four cornerstones of improving livelihood are organizing the people, building the assets of the poor, building capacity that enables women to control their own affairs and ensuring 'social security', defined in the Indian context as ensuring the necessary employment, health and child-care services without which no struggle can be sustained. Three lessons may be drawn from their example. First, organizing people is crucial to winning battles; second, alongside organized struggle, simultaneous and integrated initiatives are necessary to promote livelihoods, specifically to ensure adequate food, healthcare and employment; and third, the lines of communication with one's opponents must be kept open, even as one has to be prepared to go to court when necessary.

Government accountability

Given the existence of legal safeguards to protect the poor in India, and even to favour their advance, the fact that these are not being adequately implemented requires that the government be held accountable for doing so. Gathering and propagating information not only on legal rights, as already noted, but also on government finances, is critical. This information needs to be shared not only among oppressed groups and the general public, but also among government officials themselves, who are often ignorant of such matters. DISHA's leader, an innovator in this field, observes that politicians promise change and money each year, but never deliver. DISHA, therefore, decided to look at where the government's money was going. They conducted analyses of state budget plans, noting where commitments had been made to create particular facilities in rural areas, and then verified with local village heads whether the work had in fact been done—all too often they found it had not. Pointing out the unmet commitments through a three-day demonstration succeeded in gaining a government response. Similarly, enforcement of minimum wage laws was achieved by first informing the concerned workers and the government authorities responsible for their implementation, and then by exerting pressure so that the employers were obliged to pay as the law required them to.

In another example, Vidhayak Sansad's Centre for Budget Studies, monitoring the Maharashtra government's budgetary commitments to helping released bonded labourers become self-reliant, revealed that the state government had not allocated any amount for such work on the grounds that no incidence of bonded labour had been discovered for several years. Vidhayak Sansad produced a list of nearly 500 bonded labourers who were still awaiting the benefits due to them. If information is power, information about money, through budget analysis, is real power.

In addition to such acts of omission, there are acts of commission whereby government financing often contributes to widening the gap between the rich and the poor. In this regard, movements can play an important role in the initial stages of budget formulation, to ensure that appropriate priority is given to the needs of the poor. For example, a government may invest in dams to provide water and power that tend more often to benefit rich landowners than poor agricultural workers. The government may then say it has insufficient funds to adequately help the poor. Independent financial analysis shows, however, that alternative uses of the same funds could have dramatic impacts on poverty. Budget analysis is thus a critical tool in organizing, as is follow-up, to see where the government's money is actually going. DISHA quickly confirmed that the pattern of allocation tends to be completely in favour of the powerful. Publishing a booklet on how government monies were actually spent, and then sending the booklet to members of the assembly, bureaucracy and media, revealed the truth, and enabled the tribals, in turn, to organize around this information and demand funds for generating employment in their villages.

Organizing

Organizing the people is at the heart of virtually all the movements' approaches to empowerment for social justice. The individual leaders came to this approach by a variety of routes. In Mumbai, Vivek and Vidyullata Pandit had been university student activists, followers of socialist Jayaprakash Narayan. Vidyullata was jailed when the then prime minister, Indira Gandhi, declared a state of emergency and suspended constitutional rights in 1975. After Gandhi's subsequent defeat, the Pandits became disillusioned, as nothing really seemed to be changing, and decided to 'do the work themselves', motivated only by a basic faith in the equal rights of human beings and a dream of a world without dire poverty. Knowing little about village life, they began by establishing a training site for urban slum youths, until it soon became clear that the idea didn't work—attendance was poor and dropout rates were high. They decided instead to concentrate on goat and pig rearing projects in Vivek's home village. The villagers seemed appreciative of this work and the local landed elite helped in organizing it. Coming to recognize that these projects were welcomed in large part because they did not challenge the village's fundamental structure of inequality, the Pandits determined to focus on identifying and releasing bonded labourers, as it was their bonded status that was the root cause of their poverty. Thus they began to attack the more fundamental problem, and to acquire a broader vision— a vision of struggle to secure the economic and social rights of oppressed and marginalized people.

SEWA and DISHA started out in Gujarat, under the leadership of union organizers Ela Bhatt and M.D. Mistry, respectively. SEWA seeks 'to make [the poor] visible and give them voice', creating a variety of organizational structures that the poor people come to lead themselves and through which they increase their incomes and improve their quality of life. DISHA began by organizing tribal groups such as *tendu* leaf pickers, but soon found that their activities had to considerably broaden as they uncovered one constraint after another to improvement in the living situations of the poor. Ultimately they came upon budget analysis as a basis for broader organizing initiatives at the policy level—initiatives that have the potential to benefit ever larger numbers of the poor throughout the state.

Navsarjan, also in Gujarat, was founded by a young Dalit, Martin Macwan, who had been infuriated by the murder of NGO colleagues for attempting to organize the poor. For him, there was no other path but to fight the system that allowed this to happen. The struggle approach risks unleashing conflict and backlash, he notes; as long as power gained by the oppressed is seen to be power taken from the rich, or the relatively rich, conflict appears unavoidable. Taking one big step forward in achieving results may lead to five steps backwards if the prevailing caste or class groups seek revenge. But, like many of the movement leaders cited here, he sees no effective alternative on the path to justice. One must be prepared to risk one's life in this greater cause.

In his native Andhra Pradesh, in south India, Chennaiah was influenced by a Naxalite school teacher who instilled in him a social consciousness that led him to take up the cause of agricultural workers through leading a federation. In the same state, the leaders of the Centre for Rural Studies and Development and Asmita were similarly influenced at a young age to help the poor, notably poor women, and specifically to build an awareness of their potential and a commitment to act on that awareness.

Organizing the poor requires special leadership traits which go beyond those needed for traditional development projects. First-line leaders are dynamic personalities who bring organizations into being, mobilize members, make crucial decisions about strategy and tactics and convey a sense of purpose and action. Equally important are the second-line leaders, who form the pool of talent that supports the first-line and steps forward when new leaders are needed. Without good first-line leadership, an organization cannot grow; without good second-line leadership, it cannot last.

It may be true to some degree that leaders are born, not made—especially founders of movements. Although the first-line leaders described here come from the educated elite, the second-line has not always come from this group. Based on Indian movements experience, ideal leadership qualities include the following:

❑ Leaders have a vision, a conceptual framework, or, as they would say, an 'ideology' for what they are trying to do, and through this vision, coupled with visible personal integrity, they are able to motivate and inspire people. They challenge authority and seek action, forcing people to declare which side they are on. They do not compromise on fundamental issues.

❑ Leaders have faith in people and are able to learn from them. They are able to gain the people's confidence and support and be accountable to them. They view the leader's role as strengthening the poor to make demands, rather than as negotiating on behalf of the poor; using campaigns as opportunities to take collective action and challenge authority (including their own).

- ❏ Leaders take on difficult, controversial and risky—but critical—issues. Risk includes the possibility both of failure and of physical danger, including brutal beatings, imprisonment and even death.
- ❏ Leaders think strategically, with clarity of purpose. They assess each activity, strategy or programme in terms of how much it will strengthen the organization and further their agenda.
- ❏ Leaders are inclusive. They promote unity and solidarity within their own organizations and through collaborations, federations and spin-offs with other like-minded organ-izations.
- ❏ Leaders know how to deal with problems, resolve conflict and work with people in power. They know how to obtain, analyse, use and communicate information.
- ❏ Leaders know that change is a long-term process and they per-severe despite setbacks. They are self-critical, learn from their mistakes and adapt to changing situations.
- ❏ Most importantly, leaders create democratic institutions that will outlast them. Enablers and facilitators, rather than implementers, they build a movement, not a project. They recruit alternative leadership at every level, engaging in mentoring and promoting the confidence of all who work with them. They insist on demo-cratic decision-making, with inputs from all those affected by any given decision. They make sure that second-level cadres know what to do without day-to-day instructions.

It is worth emphasizing the need for constant focus on the funda-mental problems faced by the poor, since this focus is at the root of the uniqueness of these groups' approaches to social justice. Pigs and goats, savings and credit, childcare centres, schools and health clinics are all necessary to improve livelihoods and living conditions. But without the people's feelings of confidence and power to advocate for these on their own behalf, they risk amounting to little more than mere band-aids on an infected wound.

Special Issues in Organizing Women

The situation of women in India is particularly critical. Forced by tradition into a role of subservience to men, they have a double impediment to overcome. First, to gain the confidence and capacity to deal with men as equals, and second, to deal with the same oppressive circumstances often faced by the community as a whole. For Dalit and tribal women, the barriers are all the greater. Many women have difficulty stating their names, work and place of residence, having been identified simply by and with the men in their lives. They have been socialized to take no pride in their work and do not even consider themselves 'workers'. They are often denied education, their role seen as limited to caring for the home and children. Where women have paid employment, their wages are generally unequal to those of men and, adding insult to injury, are subsequently taken by the men and often spent on drinking or gambling.

Organizing women, therefore, has a special priority among virtually all the groups. It is in this context that one must view the SEWA story cited in Chapter Three. While the creation of a women's savings and credit mechanism could be seen as a typical NGO development project, it is important to note that the credit union was created not just for its own value, but as a tool that gave women their own institution and thus confidence in asserting themselves in a broader struggle for their due rights and needs. The fundamental problem addressed was the need for organizing, with the credit union, in this case, being one means to that end.

Working on women's issues can be particularly problematic. As experienced by leaders from Andhra Pradesh (in the experience cited in Chapter Four), women don't want to come out to meetings by themselves, fearing their husbands' reactions, often wrath. (The family may be the most dangerous place for women, given the extent of abuse and atrocities that occur in the confines of the home.) Yet, these leaders emphasized that they were not organizing women against men, but rather organizing them to understand their rights, without knowledge of which women cannot interact with men as equals. Women must be present at every level of decision-making. Systems are

> needed to monitor their participation, reservations of leadership positions must be made in favour of women, and gender policy, in general, must be a priority in all organizing efforts.

Movement leaders emphasize that there are no shortcuts to organizing. As one of them says, it takes three years to implement a project, 10 years to organize a group and 20 years to create a movement. Given the nature and extent of the problems faced by the poor in India (and elsewhere, for that matter), nothing short of a movement is likely to succeed on a sustainable basis—or, at least, that has been the experience in the worldwide environmental movement, for example, the US civil rights movement and, perhaps most to the point here, the worldwide women's movement.

The fundamental importance of organizing is emphasized here because it comes up repeatedly and in many contexts in discussions with Indian movement leaders. Without organization, there can be no ongoing progress. In the real world, where money and political power are inextricably intertwined, the poor can only break down the barriers to their progress by achieving political power of their own. Thus emerges the need for collective strength through organizing and through the power of information, particularly information on legal and budget rights. As one leader puts it,

> political action is the only way to make the poor visible and audible in India. Those born with privilege are split with those who were not. Only the privileged speak out in India. Therefore, organizing is very important to give marginalized people the strength to speak out.

Advocacy

Compared with the challenges of organizing—where the poor have been downtrodden and oppressed from time immemorial—the next step to advocacy seems somehow smaller, but it is absolutely critical if change is to occur. At one level, it is, most simply, the necessary outcome of organizing.

Advocacy consists of strategies aimed at influencing decision-making at local, state, national and/or international levels, specifically at *who decides* such matters as elections, selection of policy-makers, administrators, judges, etc.; *what is decided*— policies, programmes, laws, budgets, etc.; and *how it is decided*, in terms of the public's ready access to information and the process, extent of consultation, accountability and responsiveness of decision-makers to citizens. Effective advocacy requires a sharp understanding and analysis of a concrete problem followed by a coherent proposal for its solution.

Effective advocacy may succeed in influencing decision-making, and thus policies, by educating, or changing, policy-makers and implementers; by reforming policies, laws and budgets, or by developing new programmes; and/or by making decision-making structures and procedures more open, accountable and, in short, democratic.

Equally important is how advocacy strategies *permanently* expand the participation of citizens in decision-making and governance by educating the disadvantaged at the grassroots, so that they are able to identify and analyse problems, define their own solutions, exercise their rights and understand and use the political realm for their benefit; by building and strengthening women's and grassroots organizations, social movements and NGOs that enable disadvantaged people to present their views and demands; and by making decision-making more open and accountable to all citizens. Advocacy strategies thus have two types of objectives: *policy objectives*, in terms of what will be changed about decision-making, and *process objectives*, determining how the advocacy strategy will build citizen participation and organization.

India, of course, has the stunning example of that most successful advocate, Mahatma Gandhi, whose efforts resulted, in the end, in national independence. Most or all of the movement leaders discussed here seem to follow his precepts and example, whether consciously or not. Successful advocacy, according to them, requires a clear goal and a vision of how to achieve it, a passionate commitment to succeeding in the endeavour, a thorough understanding of power relationships and politics, a sense of strategy and timing and all the individual leadership skills listed earlier. Most importantly, while leaders from outside can contribute to the vision and long-term ideas of change, they must, through organizing, build the local people's capacity to advocate for themselves. Although it may seem easier, in a particular case, for the leader to advocate before the officials concerned, this both diminishes the impact in the short term and undercuts the power of the group for future advocacy. The people must be empowered to advocate for themselves.

On another level, a few organizations have been specifically established for the purpose of conducting advocacy on others' behalf. Using the results of research on applicable laws and/or budget analyses, they lobby within the bureaucracy, with political leaders and others as needed, while also sharing their information and efforts with the media. In these undertakings, friendly relationships with those in positions of authority and power are most helpful. What is most striking about a number of the leaders featured here is their ability to operate at multiple levels—on the one hand, with the organized power of groups of the poor behind them, they can, and do, threaten and carry out large-scale demonstrations that draw significant public attention on uncooperative officials and wealthy and higher caste oppressors. On the other hand, by virtue of what can only be understood as personal charm, augmented by persuasive knowledge and commitment, they can often negotiate quieter solutions to problems.

How have they managed to maintain good, even cordial, relations with their adversaries, even in situations of struggle?

First, using Vidhayak Sansad/Shramjeevi Sanghatna as an example, it is important to note that the word 'opponent' rather than 'enemy' tends to be used. This reflects a conscious policy emphasizing the importance of building bridges with bureaucrats, police personnel and employers—being open and transparent about one's plans and objectives, praising them when they perform justly, while being prepared to confront them when they stand in the way of justice. As Gandhi had said, 'Cooperate where you can and resist where you must'. This approach of locating the opponent in what a person does, and not in the person as such, has allowed these leaders to earn the respect of former opponents and even to turn them into allies.

Second, leaders' possession of accurate information enhances credibility when they must oppose the authorities. If there is strength in numbers, there is certainly also strength in knowledge—and in being on the side of the law.

Third, for those groups that conduct development projects, with or without accompanying movement activities, their collaboration with government and international aid programmes may be seen as a welcome display of sincerity and cooperativeness; who could argue, as cited in Chapter Three, against the desirability of a child-care centre?

Fourth, India's relatively progressive laws and its tradition of mass demonstrations and Gandhian non-violence, dating from the independence movement, create a climate where activism has to date been seen as more-or-less acceptable. Add to this an increasing worldwide focus on human rights and democracy and one sees further contextual support for partner goals.

To feel deep anger and to organize a massive demonstration, yet to do so in consultation with the very bureaucrats or employers one is opposing, is quite an achievement and no doubt helps to gain respect for movement objectives. The lesson, therefore, is a need for suppleness—for a creative and sophisticated combination of strong and principled activism, even militarism, on the one hand, and highly delicate diplomacy, on the other.

Strengthening People and Organizations

It should be clear by now that what is required to combat oppression and poverty is not only a holistic approach, but also a sophisticated and multi-faceted attitude in the people and institutions that lead the struggle. Identifying leaders and staff capable of the creative and sophisticated approaches suggested here is far from easy. In order to succeed, such leaders must be totally committed to the cause, prepared to work on behalf of the oppressed, and disposed to direct any personal power gained through their work back into the communities themselves.

This means that such individuals must be willing to resist temptations of self-promotion that may either conflict or be seen to conflict with their constituency's needs. Indeed, one of the 'hottest' topics of debate among movement leaders has revolved around whether assuming an overt political role would not provide a more powerful basis for bringing about change. One leader believes that it does, and became the head of a political party. Others, however, fear the risks of misinterpreted motivation and power corruption, and of power diminution resulting from these, and accordingly resist partisan involvement. Ela Bhatt reports that when the then prime minister, Rajiv Gandhi, invited her to join the Rajya Sabha in 1985, her SEWA colleagues, believing she could advance their cause from the parliament's upper house, urged her to accept. She recalls that in accepting the prime minister's call, 'The final question that came out of my mouth was "Do I have to join the party?" He laughed and said, "On the contrary."'

Although a greater sense of modesty may have prevented the movements' self-studies from extolling their leaders' charismatic qualities and extraordinary skills, it is clear that these lie at the root of their achievements. What is more critical to discuss at this stage, however, is the creation of second-line leadership, without which these powerful institutions could disappear, or at least lose their effectiveness, with the retirement or loss of the original founders.

A fundamental question in this regard is the extent to which leadership can be developed. Since all the founders of these groups are active in their institutions, it is impossible to be sure what will happen as and when they pass from the scene. A major thrust for virtually all of them has been leadership development in individual communities, as well as at their organizations' own managerial levels. Membership groups, such as Shramjeevi Sanghatna and SEWA, which reflect an important strength of the union and cooperative approaches, could be said to have a built-in bias for encouraging new leadership from within the groups, as their members elect leaders from among their peers in whom they presumably have confidence and respect. Others bring in and promote, based on their leadership performance and other skills, individuals from outside. Some of the leaders note that building second-line leadership in institutions demands that first-line leaders be willing to share authority—indeed, to transfer their own power and allow second-line leaders to succeed or fail on their own; without this willingness, new leadership cannot take root.

One of the groups, specifically focusing on women, frankly admits in its self-analysis that, to date, its objective of building second-line leadership had not been completely successful. They attribute this difficulty to a lack of politicization in the younger generation of women who seek employment in the development sector.

The problem with most women's groups and development groups is that there has to be commitment, political understanding and a certain professional accountability and performance. This is a combination we find hard to pass on and so fail to build a second line leadership that is satisfactory.

Interestingly, they note,

team building is also difficult because of the intense competitiveness, personal frustrations, and tensions of modern living. While the team spirit always comes up in situations of hard work and stress, it always breaks down during the normal periods of moderate activity.

This last point raises the additional and separate issue of whether the intensity needed in a struggle situation can be maintained in between specific campaign periods, and, if so, how. Several leaders emphasize that there can be no let-up; one has to continually conduct new activities, whether development undertakings or struggle causes, to keep the flame alive.

In the final analysis, the essence of empowerment is capacity-building. A relatively common mission, albeit variably nuanced, is to promote people's participation and strengthen their leadership skills and technical know-how so that the poor and oppressed are empowered to manage their own resources and take control of their lives. This same capacity must also be built into the institutions that work with them. Training thus constitutes an overarching part of movement activities.

Some organizations have been able to develop leaders from their own ranks. This is true of groups that have existed long enough to instil a sense of belonging and confidence among not only their adult members, but among the children and young people associated with them as well. SEWA has been particularly effective in this regard, with the two or three generations of young people who have grown up with SEWA as part of their lives—whether through youth camps, youth training workshops or other activities; for them, it is natural to want to participate in SEWA. In addition, the SEWA Academy provides members with training in whatever skills they seek to develop.

Another approach is to recruit college students or recent graduates as interns or as fellows with stipends. Additionally, exchange programmes can bring exposure to other groups, as can mentoring of one group by another and peer training among groups. Such methods can uncover the kind of determined, able and committed people who are ready for leadership. Such exchange can bring well-educated young people into organizations that may be rooted among the village poor, and is important as a source of second-line leaders. Only time will tell if these movements can attract talented young people in significant numbers and, if they do, whether they can effectively work with other members who may come from quite different backgrounds.

Navsarjan, for example, requires only two qualifications of new recruits: literacy and 'anger against the system'—the latter seen as a necessary prerequisite to fight for Dalit rights. Inasmuch as the average recruit for such work comes with motivations quite different from those of the founder-leader—anger aside, the employment opportunity is a key lure—training is obviously critical if one is to develop the required level of skill as well as dedication. Navsarjan then provides full-year courses for its staff, which, by the participants' own testimonies, changes their lives.

Asmita, aiming to put a gender perspective into the political discourse in the state of Andhra Pradesh, necessarily finds itself heavily engaged in consciousness-raising, followed by constant training in gender sensitization, human rights and relevant legal issues. They organize rallies reaching thousands of rural women on issues such as health and violence, women's rights, reproductive rights and political participation. They see consciousness-raising as a necessary precursor to more concrete training and capacity-building.

Training in administrative and programme skills tends to primarily come through in-house training or hired outsiders, the most effective being a combination of both. Some groups have found retired persons a good source of specific professional and technical inputs. Others use NGOs in an intermediary role, but their training often proves abstract rather than practical, focused on management rather than on organizing, and therefore not useful on the ground. Increasingly, individual leaders are taking on mentoring roles. While this assures high quality training and increases networking, it further overburdens already busy leaders; so far, however, no alternative has been found to living with the problem and striving for optimal balance.

If all the leaders place primary emphasis on capacity-building, it is perhaps because they have personally appreciated its benefits. Virtually all of them have had opportunities, often provided through the Unitarian-Universalist Holdeen India Program, for exposure to other groups' experiences, in India and abroad, including, for some, attendance at the Advocacy Institute's training programme in Washington, DC—the latter was described as having had a key, even seminal, impact on their subsequent work in India.

Alliances

Building alliances, or networking, is a critical component to enhancing one's organizational strength both in conducting campaigns and building capacity. Given the complexity of the problems faced, the need for broader knowledge and perspective and the force of numbers in asserting power, the advantage of multi-group cooperation is obvious. Groups can join forces for short- or long-term causes, but unless there is a shared vision among the component members, the alliance will be short-lived at best; at worst, it may result in power struggles, with highly negative results for the individuals and groups involved and for their struggle causes. It is important to recognize that all partners in an alliance have their own identity and legitimate power, or ego, needs, and to be honest about these. Experience suggests that members need to democratically share the responsibilities and the power, with their working framework and financial monitoring both clear and ensuring of mutual accountability. Desirably, alliances should go beyond networking with other activist groups, to forge links with academics and policy-makers in order to improve the groups' access to information and, thus, power. The Ahmedabad-based Foundation for Public Interest, which conducts research to measure the adequacy of such social services as health, sanitation and education facilities for the poor, is an example of one such institution.

If the Indian movements described here are unique in their primary focus on organizing for empowerment, they are also unique in the development of the 'institutional family' approach to meeting the need for diversity of expertise and capacity-building, while minimizing or avoiding the hazards encountered in more heterogeneous alliances or federations. SEWA founder Ela Bhatt evokes the metaphor of the banyan tree with its numerous trunks intertwining with one another, mutually reinforcing each other to build a larger whole. As noted earlier, the SEWA family is centred around the original self-employed women's union with a quarter of a million members, which has created, in turn, a number of skill-based and supporting service cooperatives around crafts promotion and marketing, agriculture, housing, banking, health and childcare, knowledge generation and national outreach.

The Vidhayak Sansad family comprises the aforementioned Shramjeevi Sanghatna, the Centre for Budget Studies, Samarthan (for policy advocacy) and, by extension, and embracing the larger advocacy-oriented community in India, the Pune-based National Centre for Advocacy Studies. The first four are mutually supporting co-organizations sharing the combined mission of securing the economic and social rights of oppressed and marginalized people. In addition, Vidhayak Sansad has provided stimulus and capacity-building guidance to a number of emerging leaders and organizations in the Marathwada area of Maharashtra, making them part of what might be described as an extended family.

In Andhra Pradesh, Asmita has extended its expertise and sense of solidarity to other groups, notably the Centre for Rural Studies and Development (CRSD).

Given the considerable challenges in starting up new institutions in the Indian (or indeed any) environment, this familial nurturing approach seems to have proven most useful, allowing newer groups to learn from the experiences of their predecessors and generally building capacities with widening ripple effects. This does not mean there are not occasional intra-familial complications or disagreements, but given the various needs for support services, capacity-building, union mobilization, etc., an important lesson from these groups' experiences is that the 'family of institutions' approach allows for maximum focus, on the one hand, and outreach and synergistic building towards societal change, on the other. Beyond this, 'exposure tours' to other organizations and meetings among movement leaders from different parts of India, as well as other countries, provide invaluable occasions for capacity-building within the extended 'family of families'. A sense of solidarity, illustrated by periodic bursts into struggle songs, is often manifest in such get-togethers, as the leaders of diverse groups find and share common causes, experiences and knowledge with one another.

Shared knowledge includes enhanced understanding of the key institutional requirements for success in their efforts. According to Indian movement leaders, these include, in brief,

☐ a strong cadre of hard-working fellow activists, seeing the work not as a job, but as a meaningful way of life;

☐ good access to, good analysis and appropriate dissemination of accurate information;

☐ good and ongoing training on many subjects, notably leadership and organizing;

☐ positive relationships with supporters and friends—and, insofar as possible, with opponents—in positions of authority and power, in the bureaucracy, media and politics, and the ability to widely advocate their cause;

☐ focus on networking, letting go of one's ego in the interest of fostering alliances for added strength;

☐ a continuing stream of objectives, issues and actions—including attention to improved livelihoods and social services—in order to sustain the movement; and finally, and perhaps most importantly,

☐ time and patience, the understanding that change takes time and that the resolution of one problem may well lead to several others; recognition that conflict is often a prerequisite to ultimate problem resolution.

It is now time to turn to the role of the donor.

8

Implications
for Donors

Arriving for the first time in New Delhi in 1962, I remember being
struck by the miserable realities of daily life in a scavenger community in Nizammudin. As manual garbage collectors, the Bhangi
people living there were treated as the lowest of the low, even by
other Dalits. That being the heyday of foreign assistance to India,
however, there was a church NGO working in the community offering relief food and training in sewing skills that could lead the
women there to better employment opportunities. Perhaps there was
hope.

Leaving India a couple of years later and returning on a visit in
the 1970s, I returned to Nizammudin, only to find exactly the same
conditions in evidence. The only difference was that a different NGO
was working there, this time on a model family planning project.

Ten years later, in the 1980s, on yet another visit, I encountered a
child sponsorship NGO operating a comprehensive community
development project emphasizing literacy and health. However, no
one came for the literacy classes, and while some came for health
care, the medicines provided could not compensate for the unsani-
tary, indeed filthy, living conditions of the neighbourhood. This project too came to an end.

In the 1990s, I was told that yet another NGO had come and started
a small savings and credit scheme in Nizammudin, but that the
people, sorely strapped for daily living expenses, had used its funds
for current consumption purposes, while continuing to go to
traditional money lenders to meet other major expenses such as

weddings and funerals. The bottom line was that over four decades, the living conditions of these people had not improved at all— nothing had changed!

Kathy Sreedhar, director of the Unitarian-Universalist Holdeen India Program (HIP), tells this story to illustrate the limitations of traditional approaches to development assistance and why HIP follows a fundamentally different approach.

HIP was formally established in 1984 through a bequest from New York lawyer and businessman Jonathan Holdeen, who designated the money for use 'in aid of maternity, child welfare, education and migration expenses' of 'natives of India and their descendents'. As the fund was being established, the Unitarian-Universalist Association invited Kathy's views on how such a fund would be most effective. An American who had married into an Indian family, Kathy had already been working on Indian development and US civil rights issues, and was thus building on knowledge gained from more than two decades of relevant personal experience. She came to some important and uncommon conclusions about how best to serve the Indian people.

> During the '60s, my social circle consisted primarily of upper-caste, upper-class British-educated Indians who were high-level civil servants, journalists, businessmen, and industrialists. Many of them were involved in designing and implementing the new government's five-year plans, intended to promote economic development and build a modern industrial state. In line with Gandhian principles learned during the Independence struggle, as well as principles based on socialism and other perspectives, many of my friends wanted to reduce some of India's terrible poverty and inequities, but they saw these goals as secondary to the main thrust of modernizing India. While a succession of five-year plans began to transform India's economic base, they left most of the population untouched. The longer I stayed in India, the more I realized that the persistence of extreme poverty and inequity derived from deeply embedded factors related to caste, class, religion, and gender. This nexus of factors defeated government plans and programs as well as the mandates of the Constitution and the more equity-oriented aspects of the laws.

Caste was officially abolished after Independence, yet remained potent, especially in rural areas where it defined social life and was critical to understanding and effecting change.

When Kathy came to the villages, the women would ask her what caste she belonged to and could not comprehend her answer—'none'. Those born outside a caste-based world cannot understand why it persists and is so powerful in shaping perceptions, and those inside it have no idea that the world can be organized any other way. Caste and privilege, or exclusion, go together. When Kathy visited projects of the Indian government, of the US Agency for International Development and of the Peace Corps, she invariably saw that it was members of the upper castes, and sometimes 'other backward castes', who captured virtually all the benefits of development programmes. It was not just that they were more powerful, as indeed they were, but that the Dalits and others simply could not imagine that they had the right to participate in the benefits of development, or the power to demand such participation.

Gender attitudes provided further obstacles. Apart from divisions between women and men, women were divided from each other too, as caste, class, religious and ethnic distinctions factored into the equation. Because India had no broad-based concept of community that crossed these divisions, the Western concept of 'community-based organization' made no sense here. In villages, for instance, different groups of people may have faced common problems but been unable to cooperate in order to jointly address them. Entrenched political and economic interests exploited the power of caste and gender to divide people and prevent any serious alteration of the status quo. It seemed clear that the politicians, civil servants, landowners, moneylenders and others at the 'upper end' of the Indian society were willing to alleviate poverty only as long as doing so did not challenge the basic structure of inequality from which they themselves benefited. Some would bribe, coerce, corrupt, even kill, to prevent real change.

The manipulation and withholding of information was crucial to the ability of the entrenched interests to protect their position. The poor had little awareness of their rights and even less access to resources or services the government had theoretically designed for them. They remained largely isolated, divided, afraid and dependent on authority—attributes, indeed, of a feudal society. They lacked voices, choices and, most importantly, the power to demand their rights or influence the decisions that affected their lives. That is why most Dalits were landless and subject to terrible social practices; why tribals and Moslems not only lived in poverty, but were discriminated against; and why women in these groups were even worse off than men were.

Large-scale government and philanthropic development efforts seldom, if ever, addressed these basic problems, nor, given their nature, could they do so. Conventional development usually operates through 'projects', which are generally top-down efforts, of limited time duration and aimed at specific tasks, such as electrifying a certain number of villages. This approach has many serious drawbacks. Projects are sectoral, focusing on one or more particular issues or problems, such as literacy, whereas human needs constitute a whole. Projects tend to be donor-driven—the donors express an interest in funding certain kinds of activities, and NGOs respond with ideas that fit those interests—an approach that often ignores the real interests of the local people, especially those who lack a voice in making decisions about the programmes that are supposed to help them. In any case, the neediest people often fail to learn about projects, whereas the well connected, who usually are in less need and relatively better off, often have the information necessary for receiving the project's benefits. Corruption in the form of bribes and kickbacks further skews the distribution of project benefits.

Kathy also observed that project-based development did not adequately take into account the Indian context. If a project is designed to enable women to save and establish credit, for example, it is important to ask what ultimate purpose the project is supposed to serve. If it is supposed to make women more independent, one must consider the social context in which the women live, so that, for example, they are not stripped of their savings by their husbands, who in rural India have almost complete control over wives. Micro-credit—even if accompanied by access to raw materials and markets, upgraded skills, a business plan, etc.—does not address the root causes of economic and gender oppression unless it works towards strengthening the people, replaces banking and credit policies that work against the poor and ensures that loan recipients, usually women, control the use of their assets and income. Any intervention must improve livelihoods on a sustainable and just basis.

Most detrimental of all, the project-based approach does not challenge power relationships. The goal of a project, such as electrifying a village, might be very worthy but might not challenge the fundamental social relationships that form the basis of exclusion and exploitation. Electricity, yes, but for whom? Related to this point is the fact that projects do not address the divisive effects of caste, and may actually reinforce a mentality of dependence by encouraging the recipients of the programmes to expect others to do things for them. If, instead, the poor would themselves demand their rights, they might learn how to analyse and solve their problems in their own way.

Kathy concluded from all this that in order to make a difference, the new Holdeen India Program had to address the inequalities of power; that is, address the issue of who makes the decisions about who uses and controls what resources and for what purposes. Economic development by itself could not lead to equity, because power inequalities skewed the distribution of economic benefits. Land reform, by itself, would not improve the lives of the poor, because when the poor did receive land, it was usually of the worst quality and they lacked the capital to make it productive. Equally large barriers existed for those who were essentially forced from the land and sought employment in government. Job reservations, or 'affirmative action', had limited success for Dalits and tribals, few of whom had the necessary primary and secondary education to take advantage of the government jobs reserved for them.

Soon after Kathy's appointment as HIP's first executive director, she visited India to formulate recommendations for optimal use of the Holdeen monies in light of this overwhelmingly difficult situation. She met with more than a hundred individuals and groups, including academics, bilateral donors, NGOs, government officials, and others, to address the problems identified in her analysis of the situation. It became clear that if the new foundation wanted to make a real difference, it would have to find suitable Indian partners capable of challenging established power relationships and enabling the excluded and exploited to demand their inclusion within society. Since conventional Indian development organizations were not prepared to do this, HIP needed to find new ones that were not tied to the old ways. Fortunately, at about this time, many activist, struggle-based Indian NGOs began to be formed, some of them seeking new approaches to the problems that had beset India since Independence. From among these, the Holdeen India Program identified the most effective partners, although it took time and experimentation.

What exactly could the new foundation do in India? Certainly it could supply funding. But for what purpose? If it wasn't going to fund projects, as conventional development organizations did, what was the alternative? After much consideration, Kathy decided that HIP should regard itself as a catalyst that would use its resources (both financial and human) to support the strengthening of leadership and capacity within Indian organizations and fill gaps that other funding sources would not or could not fill. It would support the *process* of empowerment rather than discrete development *projects*. As a catalyst for change, it would work through constantly evolving relationships with *partner organizations*, giving them access to the foundation's resources to help define problems and organize to solve them. It would seek groups that wanted to strengthen the confidence, independence and collective bargaining power of the excluded and exploited so that they could demand greater access to resources and justice and, in Gandhi's words, 'no longer play the part of the ruled'. How was this to be done? By building capacity and organizing at the grassroots—as a union, a movement, an activist organization—on the understanding that in union there is strength.

Specifically, HIP would follow seven working principles.

❑ Focus on those with the least power and fewest resources—the most excluded, marginalized and oppressed, especially Dalits and tribals, with special emphasis on Dalit and tribal *women*.

❑ Seek out leaders and groups that strengthen collective bargaining power, as well as institutions and movements through which these groups can radically improve their lives and conditions.

❑ Develop long-term partnerships with democratically governed organizations whose members own and control their institutions, resources and programmes, advocate on their own behalf, challenge unequal power relations and unjust social conditions, demand their rights and share of development, influence policies in favour of the poorest, hold the government accountable and no longer play the part of the ruled.

❑ Support collaborative, networking and mutually reinforcing activities in order to have a more broad-based impact on policies and other organizations. Each activity should strengthen the power of the organization, advance its issues and vision, and strengthen through networking the work of other like-minded organizations.

❑ Provide whatever support the groups require to strengthen their organizations and advance their issues, acting as a true collaborator in such a way that the Indian partners, not HIP, define the work to be done and the means to do it; provide support as long as the organizations and their work continue to grow.

☐ Complement funding with personal and institutional support through strategic planning, advocacy linkages and other means; non-funding support should be at least as important as grants.

☐ Keep administrative bureaucracy to a minimum in both application and implementation phases, though partners should be expected to submit satisfactory financial and programme reports on a regular basis.

Putting this agenda into place took time and experimentation. Kathy says,

In the beginning, when we were simply trying to initiate a process, we collaborated with anyone who seemed to share our aims, beliefs and vision. We looked for committed, creative, effective leaders who actually lived in the village (we tried a few who didn't live there even though they met other criteria, but that failed) and whose aim was to build a strong, united, independent, democratically run organization that could motivate and mobilize the poorest, represent their interests and translate them into action. We learned very early that we could not include the whole community in our efforts because of the way community was understood. In India the concept of 'community' usually excludes, by definition, the people who are our partners—the traditional power hierarchy would not allow this. Furthermore, the prestige and position of the elite are so great that when the 'community' is addressed as a whole, the non-elite elements do not participate and invariably defer to the elite. Women, Muslims, tribals and Dalits are so oppressed that they must be strengthened before joining the whole.

We had particular difficulty addressing issues that affected women, because there were few grassroots women's groups and it was socially unacceptable for single women activists to enter the villages. In consultation with a number of institutions and individuals, we did manage to identify a variety of types of groups as working partners. Some focused on Dalits or tribals, and a few said they were interested in women's development, but usually they were limited to traditional development approaches and led by men. Within the year, I had learned that women were too often marginalized or 'projectized' in these organizations, and we have not supported such organizations since.

Without these NGOs we needed to find alternative ways of reaching women. We found some very effective husband–wife teams prepared to work in villages, and we also began supporting struggle groups of Dalits and tribals, even though they had no women's agenda, in the hope that as they grew stronger they would have the confidence and strength to act on issues they might not have seen as important in previous years. We are beginning to see significant developments with organizations that we have been working with for years. In Maharashtra, we have been working closely for nine years with groups of Dalits who have been fighting against untouchability and for land reform and a minimum wage. They had no women in decision-making positions until recently, but in 1999, they brought to one of our meetings in India the most extraordinary cadre of women leaders.

The initial collaborative efforts provided the opportunity to test assumptions and modes of working. Out of this came a decision to focus HIP's support on struggle groups—collections of persons who organize for joint action to address an issue they have defined and want to remedy. Kathy looked to the dominant Indian model of struggle groups—labour and trade unions, which historically were one of the powerful expressions of popular will and collective action. Once she imagined HIP as engaged in supporting struggle groups, it was possible to define a clear role that the organization could play, and give real meaning to words and phrases that had gradually been turned into clichés and jargon by the development establishment.

In a union, as Kathy has noted, solidarity comes from each individual's perception that group action is the best way to achieve goals. The commitment of each union member—as expressed in the payment of dues, attendance at meetings, participation in strikes and demonstrations, and voting in union elections—is the bottom-up bond that gives successful unions the power they need to confront entrenched interests. The effectiveness of some unions in India suggested that the bottom-up, movement-based approach was by far the most likely to produce significant and sustainable change for the poor and oppressed.

Words such as 'empowerment' and 'participation' were seen to take on new meaning, beyond the lip service they usually receive, when considered in light of the bottom-up approach. Now, even the most excluded people could become subjects and actors in the struggle to improve their lives. In conventional parlance, empowerment usually implies that one person gives power to another, without reference to the structure that prevents the powerless person from using that power. But the bottom-up approach means gaining and exercising power at all levels and in all spheres, including the household, the village, the market and the government. The process of gaining power includes building awareness and confidence, and developing analytic, organizing and problem-solving skills, as well as strategic actions for change and the capacity to transfer skills to other powerless persons. In other words, it involves strengthening groups of people rather than attempting to do 'projects'.

'Participation' is another buzzword that takes on new meaning when associated with the bottom-up approach. Now it can mean not merely agreeing to decisions but actually making them. For example, *panchayat* training is very popular in today's India. The *panchayat* is the traditional village council and is important in the lives of the village residents. Efforts to train women, Dalits and tribals who have been elected to *panchayats* through reservations (affirmative action) have begun. Admirable as this sounds, experience suggests that it only works when an outside organization comprising these groups supports the newly elected members. Otherwise, how can one expect a landless labourer to disagree with a landlord on whom he may depend for his survival? Similarly, there are many instances of women being elected to *panchayats* but not uttering a word at the council meetings because it is traditionally the husband who makes the decisions; and of Dalits being elected *sarpanch* (head of the *panchayat*), and sitting at the feet of the upper caste people.

HIP's determination to work through a bottom-up approach and to avoid objectifying its partners as 'recipients' or 'beneficiaries', led it to operate through peer, collegial relationships with the partners. This required considerable self-examination and effort, because funding relationships are inherently unequal. As Kathy says,

Nonetheless, I believe the philosophy we have developed at HIP minimizes the inherent drawbacks and maximizes effectiveness. The key is to always ask, 'Who is setting the agenda? Who is deciding what aspects of a given organization, union or group are being expanded or enhanced—the members or the funder?' If the former, the relationship is probably peer-based. Without a peer-based relationship, the 'partnership' will exist only as a public fiction.

Of course, every foundation or development organization has its interests and concerns, and to that extent *any* support can be viewed as embodying an extraneous element that may distort the recipient's activities. The more valid question, however, is the extent of donor intervention in the workings of a recipient organization. To the extent that the donor prefers to contribute to specific projects of an organization, it risks imposing its own views on the recipient group, perhaps unwittingly, through the well known phenomenon whereby recipients adjust their activities to match the available funding. Over the long term, such adjustments can impair a group's ability to function independently and in the true interests of its members or beneficiaries. This has happened among at least one group of HIP partners lured by a European NGO to projectize and overextend their activities, realizing too late the costs in terms of lost effectiveness.

HIP tries to limit its extraneous impact on partners by operating in peer relationships that rest on consensus. In Kathy's words, 'we try to practice the same qualities with our partners that we expect of them with their members or constituents. This means a shared vision and conceptual framework. Partners, especially those who are advocates rather than development professionals, need to know what we believe, which side we are on. In fact, they introduce me (and HIP) as an advocate, not a funder'—a notable and highly significant distinction.

To be effective in this context, Kathy has found it important to have a personal as well as professional relationship with HIP partners, to know each other's families, live in each other's homes, share jokes, songs, celebrations. Indeed, she is considered by many of the partners as a real family member, an older sister who challenges, cajoles, sometimes teases, and inspires. In the annals of 'foreign aid', her status with HIP's partner leaders is definitely unique. Anticipating the question that inevitably follows, Kathy feels certain that

Such relationships do not preclude objectivity; indeed, they make it easier to accept the probing and questioning as to goals, strategies, decision-making, capacity-building and follow-up that may be our most important role. We constantly challenge our partners to focus on the relationship between the overall goals they pursue and the activities that will achieve them. Otherwise, the group may focus on activities as an end in and of themselves, as if the point were simply to complete the assigned tasks rather than to address fundamental change. We try to avoid a common failing of funders, who too often focus on inputs rather than outputs, on activities rather than impact.

HIP's insistence on genuine partnership led in early 2000 to the creation of a five-member India Committee chaired by SEWA's Ela Bhatt and including leaders of several of the movements described in this book. While avoiding potentially sensitive involvement with individual grant proposals, they play a critical role in giving general policy guidance to HIP's director and the members of the US-based Advisory Board, including the Unitarian-Universalist Association, which has the overall responsibility for the programme.

Most donors see themselves as funding institutions. HIP sees itself as much more than that. Its Indian partners seem to agree that HIP's use of complementary support—such as information, contacts, expertise, vision and even passion—is as vital as money for increasing their visibility, reputation, effectiveness and ability to influence policy change. From the beginning, HIP has tried to be flexible, responsive and willing to 'do the needful' to strengthen organizations in changing times and contexts. In some cases, this has meant filling gaps that other sponsors have not. For example, when Navsarjan received a large grant to expand its work in districts in Gujarat, but received no funds for vehicles to enable such expansion, HIP provided the money for the vehicles. When SEWA received a grant to buy computers but not to train staff in their use, HIP provided the training funds. In other cases, doing the needful has meant risk-taking—seed money for a new venture that no one else will fund or start-up funds for a leader wanting to form a new group. Since HIP grants are designed to meet the needs of its partners, they are used for different purposes at different times, depending on what is most useful for building capacity and organization. Success often elicits counter-reactions and a backlash that may bring some efforts to a halt. This can require a change in how HIP's support is given, such as by placing greater emphasis on strategic planning, advocacy linkages, or by other means. Flexibility is the key.

As groups develop their leadership potential and demonstrate an ability to act effectively, HIP helps make them known to other groups in India and to foundations, organizations and the media abroad. Publicity and personal connections of this sort are important aspects of developing a group's visibility, and have the additional virtue of providing a platform for representatives of partner organizations to speak to new audiences. They have also attracted other foundations and thus enabled HIP to leverage about US$ 10 million by inspiring such donors to collaborate in partner efforts. In addition, HIP has promoted two-way exchange between its Indian partners and other international organizations—Asia Society, Institute for Women's Global Leadership, Human Rights Watch, Advocacy Institute, Center for Budget and Policy Priorities—and at international conferences sponsored by the United Nations, Association of Women in Development (AWID), International Development Conference (IDC), and others. HIP nominates individuals from partner organizations for prestigious awards such as the Robert F. Kennedy Human Rights Award and the Eisenhower Fellowship in the United States, and for international honours such as the Anti-Slavery International Award.

HIP has also supported, through individual partners, issue-based campaigns such as the National Campaign on Dalit Human Rights and SEWA's successful international campaign to gain ILO recognition of home-based workers. Dalit groups have recently gained wide public awareness, not just in India but around the world, and now constitute a movement, communicating with each other, arranging to work in concert and building their capacity both as individual groups and collectively. Complementary support activities like these cost more in time than in money, and enable HIP to multiply the impact of its limited resources.

HIP realized early on that developing a critical mass among organizations greatly increased the effectiveness of the organizations and thus also of the support that HIP provided. A strategic decision was made to focus most of the programme's attention on a well-defined region consisting of the states of Gujarat, Rajasthan, Maharashtra, Madhya Pradesh and Andhra Pradesh. At one time, HIP supported groups in other parts of India, but site visits and communication became too difficult and not cost-effective. Funding scattered groups solely because they were deserving was not enough to force deep-seated change, because experience showed that when groups act singly they cannot maximize on political and social pressure. Many Dalit groups are now part of a national movement because of their sustained efforts to communicate with each other, arrange to work in concert, reinforce each other, exchange ideas, build their capacity and continually strengthen their solidarity as groups and as a movement. This did not come about by accident. Both HIP and the groups have consciously worked in this direction, patiently over many years, to achieve noteworthy results.

Because of its belief in the need for critical mass, HIP encourages its partners to establish working relationships with each other and with other groups, whether through federations, issue-based campaigns, regional groupings or networks. Having learned by experience, HIP now works only with groups already connected with existing partners or those prepared to do so. There are different types of collaboration. Some involve mentoring of one organization by another, others the exchange of skills or services. Some are federations of small groups collaborating as 'families', such as the 18 to 20 groups in Marathwada (in Maharashtra) that are collaborating with the Rural Development Centre and are mentored by Vidhayak Sansad. The SEWA family mentors other SEWAs, such as the Gujarat Mahila Housing Trust, SEWA Bank and SEWA Bharat, as well as other women's groups. CECOE-DECON attempted to play such a role vis-à-vis the Dedwana salt worker group and other local entities in its Rajasthan network, albeit less successfully in terms of empowerment than originally hoped. Beyond the inherent advantages in terms of mutual learning, capacity-building and strength in numbers, such collaborative relationships can be helpful in channelling outside funding as well. Many foreign donors find it logistically complicated to support a multiplicity of small groups, preferring to channel their aid through larger entities instead.

In short, collaboration can very effectively leverage skills and resources. It enables the Centre for Budget Studies, for example, to gather and analyse crucial information about the state and federal budgets, and then distribute it to those groups that can best use it in their efforts to force the government to spend money as allocated—a process that only works if people are connected and are accustomed to sharing information. There is, as well, an element of capacity-building here, since organization staff must have the skill to find the information, analyse it carefully and present it to partners and collaborating organizations in a timely and accurate manner.

Although HIP encourages its partners to collaborate in any way possible, this does not always work as intended. The relationship of a large organization with a small one can raise delicate issues of control. One of HIP's earliest efforts, for example, involved a large and established organization in Gujarat which provided assistance to a small new group of Dalits who had been displaced by a dam project and were seeking their land back. The larger group was overly controlling of the relationship and prevented the smaller one from interacting with other groups, which made the new organization totally dependent and unable to grow.

HIP has also come to learn the limitations of networking. From the beginning, networking was encouraged as an efficient and effective way to spread information and establish contacts among groups, but experience showed that while loose networks can grow and spread quickly and efficiently, tightly organized ones run the danger of developing coordinating superstructures with lives of their own, often replicating the same entrenched, hierarchical structures found in the society at large. Overall, HIP's experience suggests that networks which function as *movements* work best.

Through its own networking, HIP's influence has been well in excess of its limited resources. In addition to its conscious efforts to leverage other donor funds for partner movements, the broader networks through which these movements have collaborated have had considerable impact. The National Campaign for Dalit Human Rights, for example, used a Human Rights Watch book, *Broken People*, and *60 Minutes*, a TV programme in the United States, to advocate for its agenda.

Advocacy may now be something of a fad in India, but it was not always so. HIP's small start with bringing eight leaders to participate in the Washington, DC-based Advocacy Program in 1989 grew in subsequent years to give more than 60 Indian leaders the opportunity to meet and talk with US advocacy groups. It also led to the creation of the National Centre for Advocacy Studies and several other institutions for advocacy training in India that have greatly raised the profile of this critical activity in the country. One result of this advancement is that many Indian NGOs have begun engaging in advocacy efforts. Not all, to be sure, define advocacy in the manner intended here; some limit their definition to the signing of petitions against child labour, for example, without going on to take the more serious risks of literally *demanding* action by filing charges and courting potential reprisals. The questions to be asked are, 'Advocacy to what end?' and 'Will this advocacy lead to empowerment of the oppressed?'

HIP and its partners have also been pioneers in the technique of budget analysis as a tool for pressuring, shaming or suing governments into honouring their legal commitments to excluded and exploited groups. This technique, which HIP brought to India through its Advocacy Fellows Program, is now entering the mainstream philanthropic world. The Ford Foundation hosted the first Indian National Workshop on Budget Analysis and Policy Advocacy in Goa in 1999, the International Conference on Budgets and Poverty in Mumbai in 2000, and workshops on budget analysis for partners in the former Soviet Union and in Africa. Budget analysis has spread to over 40 countries as an advocacy tool.

The business of donors addressing poverty and oppression has a long history of 'magic bullets'. Community development, agricultural extension, literacy and primary education, family planning, land reform and micro-credit have all had their turn. The current fads are advocacy, participation and empowerment, and it is possible to see HIP and its partners simply as practitioners of these fads. But there is a clear difference between the HIP approach and most others. HIP uses loaded words such as 'empowerment' and 'participation' in their most literal sense, truly leaving decision-making power in the hands of its partners rather than its own. As suggested in the partner stories told here, this approach has been proven to work, and should work for other foundations and organizations willing to consider alternative options.

Not all of HIP's efforts have succeeded. 'Projectized' women's activities frequently proved ineffective in empowering women in any long-term, comprehensive or meaningful way. Small groups supported by HIP often didn't make it, lacking either the necessary quality of leadership or critical mass, or both. Sometimes groups have been lured by large grants from other donors and have over-extended their ability to perform, not to mention their focus on the empowerment approach. In some settings in India, such as those where the overall threshold of violence is very low, the forces opposing change are simply too strong to permit success; a modicum of respect for the law is a necessary prerequisite for change.

HIP and its partners regard their approach as a work in progress, which must always change to stay current and relevant. As Kathy puts it,

> Our partners and we have made a beginning but we still have a lot to learn. Our mission requires that we help create a 'culture of questioning'. Everyone, the elite and marginal groups, lives in an environment steeped in deference and adherence to one's familial and inherited position. What makes our partners different is that they have broken the 'culture of obedience', and question the existing structures that determine their own lives. A Dalit woman who has broken out of seeing the world in traditional ways has achieved greater self-determination than an educated, middle class Indian who accepts the traditional values unthinkingly.
>
> By the same token, we at HIP must constantly question our assumptions and our methods, to keep our field of vision clear and broad and open to possibilities. For example, how can our partners and we change traditional ways of thinking and, hence, of operating? How can we develop systematic, strategic training programs that reach large numbers of people and are customized to meet individual and group needs? Who can do the training and, more important, train the trainers? Is there an effective way to operate in the context of adverse factors over which the group has no control (for example, backlash, lack of government clearance to receive foreign donations, rise of communalism, government cutbacks of social welfare and service programs)? How long do groups require to grow and change? How can we come to grips with the conflict that can arise between producing short-term results and organizing for change over the long term? We continue to grope for answers to questions like these, and try to come closer to answering them.

In addition to these issues, HIP must pay attention to its own infrastructure and future evolution. The programme has been exceptionally dependent, since the beginning, on the unique person, and personality, of Kathy Sreedhar as director. While the US-based Advisory Board and the new India Committee play important roles, aside from part-time administrative support,

Kathy Sreedhar *is* HIP. There are advantages to this highly personalized approach—bureaucracy is at an absolute minimum, a point highly appreciated by HIP's Indian partners—but the disadvantage in terms of overdependence on the charismatic leader, with no second-line leadership yet in view, is embarrassingly obvious. Pressed to respond to this concern, those associated with HIP indicate that a new director will be appointed a year before Kathy ultimately steps down, thus allowing for extensive training and interaction with the India partners and their work. As with the Indian movements described in the preceding chapters, however, the extent to which positive momentum can be sustained over several decades, as leaders come and go, has yet to be seen.

The bottom line, however, is clear. 'What is critical,' says Kathy, 'is that the vulnerable must be able to protect themselves; the dependent must learn to be independent; the isolated must join in common struggle; and the fearful must gain confidence through joint action with others.' The struggle to achieve this continues.

The Woman Who Asks a Thousand Questions

Susan P. Willens*

It is evening in poverty-stricken Marathwada, India, on the campus of the Campaign for Human Rights. A crowd of 300 activists gathers under a green and saffron tent, singing, listening to speeches and performing comic skits in which Untouchables confront cruel landlords with hilarious results.

* Dr Willens teaches English at The George Washington University in Washington, DC. The trip described here was her first visit to India. This article previously appeared in 'Monday Developments', InterAction's newsletter, in July 2001.

Ordinarily these young men and women live in surrounding villages and towns among the people they serve. This evening, some walked in from the 'shack schools' where they teach the children of migrant workers. Others bounced over rutted roads in jeeps from courtrooms where they represent villagers who lose their land or suffer caste violence and police brutality. Still others hitchhiked from government offices where they argue for needed electricity, water or roads.

They came to thank Kathy Sreedhar, the small, sixty-something American woman whose support of the Campaign helps make their work possible. So they intersperse the singing and clowning with tributes and gifts to her. Because I am traveling with Kathy, my lifelong friend, I receive a scarlet sari from these generous hosts. My best gift, though, is the chance to observe how Kathy does her work as the director of a small development organization, the Holdeen India Fund of the Unitarian-Universalist Church.

For 18 years Kathy has travelled to India two or three times a year, pursuing her vision of international funding for social change. She works with people, not with projects. She invests money and time in just a few organizations. Each of her groups determines its own goals and methods. Although I am a newcomer to the theory of international funding, I know I am seeing a revolutionary at work.

How can a Western donor with a staff of one secretary and only $750,000 a year to give away help fight gigantic human rights battles? First, she finds charismatic leaders who confront injustice with anger, as she does. She says, 'Since I was old enough to recognize it, injustice makes me furious!' Powered by that fury, Kathy recognizes soul brothers and sisters in the Indian human rights movement and encourages them to tackle the difficult issues.

So the activists have ideals. Next they need organization, staff, skills, direction and funds to realize them. Kathy supports them financially, befriends and consults with them, cajoles, berates, suggests, and connects them with each other and with training in India, Europe and the US. Her most powerful tool is questions. In meetings with her groups, often lasting over several days, Kathy asks thousands of questions, aiming to clarify what each organization wants and needs to do.

In Marathwada, for example, I sit in on several days of Kathy's meeting with Eknath, the director of the Campaign for Human

Rights. Handsome in his white tunic and trousers, with a full white beard and sparkling eyes, Eknath has worked in this hard-scrabble region for a dozen years, gradually establishing a presence among the workers in the sugarcane fields and brick kilns. Kathy meets with him for hours, asking questions: What do the villagers want most? What are the major challenges? How will you manage the schools you want to establish? What changes in staffing must you make? Can you find time for training at the advocacy institute in Mumbai? What pressures do you feel from funders?

In response, Eknath pours out his fears, his achievements and his plans. Together they hammer out a new organizational structure for Campaign for Human Rights. Kathy is more than a funder, she is a co-traveler.

I first heard the term 'co-traveler' from Vivek Pandit, Eknath's associate and an effecitve creator of social change through his union Vidhayak Sansad in Mumbai. Vivek has worked closely with Kathy for 12 years. He is a hero. He has saved more than a thousand bonded labourers from slavery in Maharashtra state and has established hundred of schools for ex-untouchable and tribal children there. He says of Kathy, 'She gives us much more than money. She is a co-traveler. My work is everywhere and she is everywhere with me. Other funders look only at the budget; she gives me liberty. It is unique. She really cares about justice inside of herself. That gives me courage to keep on fighting.'

As darkness falls over the multicolored tent, the activists praise Kathy because she cares. Her work is up close and personal, responsive to the needs of the Indian leaders and organizers who take the risks. By asking questions to help them structure their work, Kathy makes sure 'her' groups realize their huge dreams for a just society in India.

9

Concluding Thoughts

Amongst the vast array of organizations and movements seeking change in and amelioration of the human condition, some have done so through *'development'* and others through *political action.* The former come from a long tradition of social welfare found in most societies—sometimes linked to religious associations, sometimes secular, but inevitably comprised of those concerned with the well-being of the less fortunate people among them. India has had a particularly rich tradition of this, especially in the Independence and post-Independence periods, when social workers have enjoyed a respected status within the social and cultural system. In recent decades, many such workers have expanded their scope beyond immediate, short-term relief and welfare to development activities capable of sustaining themselves over time. These have included investments in income-generating small enterprises, growing more food and, in the words of the proverb, teaching the poor how to catch more fish.

Those seeking change through political action have generally concluded that little of enduring value can be achieved by operating through the existing power structures and, therefore, they have sought to overthrow it. Although they may be fully as altruistic as social welfarists, their style of operation, not to mention their underlying assumptions, is different. Rarely, at least in modern India, have the two approaches been combined together. In Vivek Pandit's words,

Till recently, there has been an either/or situation between NGOs and People's Organisations. Both have kept away from each other for various reasons. NGOs have termed People's Organisations as being 'political' and unnecessarily engaging with the State in confrontations instead of working for the 'development' of the community. People's Organisations on the other hand have termed NGOs as 'status-quoist' and as 'bandaging the wound without addressing the cause of the disease'.

All too often, well-meaning NGOs have believed that good deeds are by definition good, almost ignoring the question of whether they actually result in lasting self-reliance, human rights and a sense of human dignity for those assisted. In the words of the Dalit Solidarity Network, 'many NGOs ... lack proper perspective, policies and strategies and their approach is poverty-centered rather than rights-based. As a result the status quo of Dalits is maintained and discrimination and human rights violations of Dalits continues.' Similarly, groups focusing on political change have too often given inadequate attention to ensuring that the desired human outcomes at individual and community levels accompany political changes.

This book has cited a handful of groups that explicitly recognize, and act on, the mutually reinforcing necessity of both development *and* political action approaches—recognizing also, however, that political change is clearly the primary requisite in order to ensure that development benefits accrue to those most in need. They define political action not in party terms, but in terms of gaining access to resources and lawful rights. They organize the poorest and the most marginalized people to challenge the inequality in power relationships, so that they may take control of their own lives and make decisions for themselves.

Their success has influenced others. The work of Vidhayak Sansad in Maharashtra, to mention one example, inspired bonded labourers in Nepal to demonstrate for their rights, leading the national government to free all such labourers in 2000. SEWA is another organization that has gained so much international recognition and emulation that it has effectively exported its concept to every continent where women home-workers and street vendors are organizing and demanding better pay, better working conditions and a say in how their work and lives are organized. The message for these women is the same that SEWA has brought to millions of Indian women—organization brings power, and power can fundamentally change lives.

Given the compelling evidence in its favour, why is a combined empowerment and development approach not more common? There are many reasons, no doubt, not the least of which are the difficulties inherent in implementation, some of which are listed here.

First, as should be apparent in the case examples cited in the previous chapters, such organizations require exceptionally sophisticated, charismatic and courageous leadership. Exceptional people, by definition, are in short supply in the world, particularly considering the need for an accompanying degree of ego control that allows them to truly listen to the oppressed and to cooperate with others, curbing any temptation to amass personal, as opposed to group, power. The leaders described here are invariably well educated men and women, mostly from urban, higher caste, middle class backgrounds. Some were associated with development organizations but felt frustrated by the limitations to their effectiveness and thus sought to apply themselves to action groups.

The supreme challenge for these leaders is to shift over their power to local groups of the oppressed, transitioning their role to an essentially catalytic one. This requires of them the further ability to identify new leadership among non-elites as well. One of them says,

> Anyone who is uncomfortable with the present situation and is ready to take risks and work hard to change it can be a leader. It does not require literacy, university degrees, good looks or great skills of articulation. Someone who speaks well, writes well, is well read and is good looking, but does not stand by the people in action cannot be called a leader. The only test of leadership is action.

Second, success depends on achieving critical mass. The strength of the poor, their ability to gain bargaining power, lies in numbers. While institutional stability is necessary, struggle movements must simultaneously aim for growth; they must be active, dynamic, constantly responding to changing conditions, always seizing opportunities. They are institutionally strongest when they are expanding—whether in terms of number of members, territorial extent, political influence or other criteria of success. Failure to do so may result in the kind of passivity that has been so deadening to efforts at social change. If a group cannot quickly increase its own membership under a dynamic leader, it must join with other groups to be effective. To quote one leader, 'A movement must move or lose.'

Third, capacity-building and training are critical. While movements must grow, they must also maintain internal cohesion and group solidarity—not always an easy combination. Constant training is one way to ensure this, as well as to ensure that appropriately qualified people undertake the difficult task of empowerment. Training is a hugely important requirement, even as it taxes the inevitably limited number of individuals who have the necessary talents, sensitivities and leadership qualities to carry it out. Follow-up is also critical, and too often ignored. To offer a training course is only the beginning; trainees also need long-term mentoring by the most experienced and skilful leaders available, as well as opportunities to observe comparable successful activities through exposure visits, staff exchanges, workshops, and the like.

Fourth, Time! A major reason that development projects too often fail to achieve their intended objectives is that unreasonable timeframes are set for doing so. Civilization and human patterns as we know them have evolved over millennia, but it is hard for well-meaning individuals with professional career spans of a few decades, operating within artificial demarcations of five-year plans or three-year funding cycles, to accept that meaningful change takes longer than they might wish. While impatience in seeking empowerment can well be a virtue and can hasten the process, realism, a reasonable level of patience and understanding and a long-term plan are critical to the process of achieving self-sustaining empowerment.

Fifth, appropriate resources are necessary. The reality, however, is that, with a few exceptions, local elites—those who have the resources to help—cannot be expected to support efforts likely to erode their own power. Furthermore, while government agencies fund some of the development activities of the organizations discussed here, it is not surprising that efforts that involve lobbying the bureaucracy to implement government laws do not receive government support. This means that foreign donors have key roles to play, since it is primarily their funds that permit the organizations a degree of freedom of action. In fact, funds are not the only resource needed; experience, ideas, a sense of solidarity and networking are also key, though often neglected, resources that organizations require in order to be effective.

Sensitivity in how resources are brought to bear is important. Those who would help are often unaware of the true nature and roots of the problems they observe. To say this is not necessarily an indictment of their intelligence, given the complexity of the issues involved and the generally parochial contexts of class-defined socialization processes in schools and home environments in the course of growing up. Equally understandable is the resistance of the elites, or even of the merely relatively better off, to engaging in political action to strengthen the poor at their own expense; vested interests have always been opposed to change. Further complicating the situation is an often complex web of institutional and bureaucratic regulations that permeate a seemingly omnipresent government, limit flexibility and also impede the prospects for change.

These factors inhibit the ability of domestic and foreign NGOs alike to respond as sensitively to issues of empowerment as needed, and to be effective in doing so. There are differences, of course, between domestic and foreign donors, quite aside from the fact that the latter generally enjoy access to substantially larger resources. The most obvious is that foreign NGO representatives are likely to have less first-hand familiarity with the national and local cultures of a place, and with appropriate ways of operating within the foreign society and bureaucracy. Having said this, however, their status outside the local social system may simultaneously provide them with a cleaner slate upon which to base a more objective understanding of local realities—unswayed by the prevailing caste and class system in India, for example—and the inevitably parochial limitations of any culture's socialization process. Furthermore, their relative immunity as outsiders to the cause of local vested interests affords greater flexibility of action, limited only by any nationalistic sensitivities expressed over the perceived dangers of foreign influence. Yet foreign influence has also proven effective in strengthening the hand of human rights initiatives through its potential to generate international publicity and lend powerful support from outside the country. In general, therefore, and while recognizing that any generalization is fraught with exceptions, international NGOs can—if they are sufficiently sensitive—play an important role in fostering grassroots empowerment movements.

Despite their potential to do so, international NGOs are often stymied in their work by the very nature of their own support bases, principally in Europe and North America. The NGOs' supporters are often fearful, or at least chary, of 'getting involved in politics', not recognizing that anything they do will in fact have political consequences. All too many 'humanitarian' development interventions lend support to the status quo in power relationships and therefore perpetuate elite control over the poor and oppressed.

Besides this, American and European NGO supporters generally expect to see visible results and verifiable accomplishments from their contributions—such as numbers of wells dug, schools and clinics constructed and micro-credit loans granted—not to mention the impact achieved with these inputs, which are hard enough to discern. How, then, can one visualize or assess the results of empowerment? How can one measure it? As the case stories in this book suggest, 'outputs' here have more to do with psychological and political shifts that will, in turn, produce measurable improvements in quality of life. But the process is, in the first instance, just that—a *process*; and the timetable is invariably long—longer than virtually any NGO or other donor is generally willing to wait, given the imperatives of satisfying individual contributors a continent or more away.

HIP, for one, is spared this double onus, thanks to its status as a foundation immune to the need to constantly seek funds from the general public. It can thus provide general and unrestricted support, placing full trust in the wisdom and honour of its Indian partners and sharing with them the risks of possible setbacks or failures. An important lesson of the HIP experience is the necessity of working with groups in which one feels comfortable placing the requisite trust, of working intimately with them, not in the typical style of donors but rather as solidarity colleagues, prepared to minimize bureaucratic requirements and limitations and allow free rein to the group's conduct of its empowerment mission.

Admittedly, this is no easy task. The number of truly effective leaders and groups is limited, as the Holdeen experience has itself confirmed. It is perhaps unrealistic to expect either that all donor assistance be given in the style recommended here or that all such partnerships be as seemingly egalitarian and mutually satisfactory as those represented in these pages. But, surely, much more can be done in this direction, and with time, a spiralling increase in opportunities is certain to develop from the examples set and synergies developed. As always—among donors, in this case—enlightened leadership is key; the kind of leadership that can with equal dexterity promote meaningful partnerships with effective empowerment movements in India and elsewhere, and educate the donors' own European and American constituencies on the critical importance of supporting these movements.

The extent to which both empowerment movements and their international partners can be successful and influential in the long run depends, in turn, on the extent to which innovative leadership is developed on an ongoing basis. While the original founders of several of the Indian groups described here have already stepped down from daily operating responsibilities, their continuing presence on the scene makes it difficult to judge whether the emerging new leadership, now successful, will remain successful in the long run. Certainly, the original Gandhian movement has lost its lustre, at least as a discrete organized force. On the other hand, individuals influenced by Gandhi or, more recently, by the esteemed Gandhian, Jayaprakash Narayan, have taken up their own forms of the cause, including several featured in these pages. It may well be, therefore, that excessive emphasis should not be placed on whether each individual organization or movement can attract the necessary second- and third-line leadership to continue intact through the ages. Rather, it may be sufficient to assume that, as has happened in the past, new leaders will indeed arise, within these movements and elsewhere, inspired by the influence of the leaders described here. Regardless of whether the Navsarjans or the DISHAs continue forever, it is almost certain that at least a few members of the oppressed groups with which they now work will continue the cause as they discard their shackles and capture the ability to fight for their own rights in the future.

A few will no doubt come to found their own movements for human rights and social justice—some of them, perhaps, in places far afield from those of their predecessors. One has only to look at the example of Dr Martin Luther King, Jr, whose non-violent movement to empower American black people was inspired by Gandhi, whereupon King himself later added to the inspiration for new empowerment movements in India. *We Shall Overcome,* the moving anthem of the American civil rights struggle, is sung around the world today.

Ideally, great leaders should influence international donors as well, as part of a mutually reinforcing solidarity in struggle. This is an important further lesson to be derived from the experience of the Holdeen India Program, as its leaders' views have been shaped by, as much as they themselves have shaped, those of their Indian partners. HIP is not alone in this regard, as other donor foundations and NGOs are also increasingly espousing similar empowerment approaches. Such reciprocal learning inevitably results in a level of experience and knowledge that exceeds the sum of its parts, snowballing in Indian and Western donor circles even as it then spreads around the world.

The power of example has influenced the spread of great ideas and thus moulded human history since time immemorial. So too, hopefully, will the experiences, successes and failures, and lessons learned here contribute to more successful efforts to empowering the oppressed, wherever they may be, to live new lives of freedom, prosperity and dignity.

Appendix 1

Organizational Profiles

1

Vidhayak Sansad

Director: *Vidyullata Pandit*

(Established in 1979)

Purpose

To work for overall development of rural areas, particularly to meet the needs of education, health and income generation of rural people.

Overall Approach and Strategy

- ❏ Organize tribals, Dalits, women, and others below poverty line, and train them to struggle for their rights through non-violent means and to use techniques of advocacy against exploitation, injustice and violation of rights
- ❏ As a supplement and complement to the above, conduct specific activities such as agricultural development, watershed development, training of local leaders, use of state budget to ensure government accountability

Major Programmes

- ❏ In conjunction with its partner union, Shramjeevi Sanghatna, which helped bring about the release of over 1,500 bonded labourers, Vidhayak Sansad has worked towards the rehabilitation of released bonded labour by starting such initiatives as agricultural, brick kiln and fishing cooperatives, and poultry and pisciculture programmes.

◻ As the Sanghatna has worked to return the alienated land of the weaker sections back to the rightful owners, Vidhayak Sansad has organized development programmes designed to increase agricultural yields.

◻ As Sanghatna members and the children from the oppressed sections were fighting with the government to implement an Education Guarantee Scheme for children aged 6–14 years, who are unable to avail of their right to education because they have to take care of their younger siblings, look after the cattle or work as labourers, Vidhayak Sansad started its campaign to secure children's right to education and began running 60 schools for the children of migrant brick kiln labourers, 53 special schools for out-of-school children aged 9–14 years and 10 hamlet schools.

◻ Vidhayak Sansad operates the Centre for Budget Studies, which analyses the state budget and passes the resultant information to people's representatives in the state legislative assembly, to use as a tool in arguing for policy changes.

Type of Organization

Vidhayak Sansad is a society–public trust which works very closely with Shramjeevi Sanghatna, a trade union of some 15,000 members registered in 1982.

Governance and Decision-making

Policy-level programme and financial decisions are made by the executive committee of the organization while programme details are decided by the project heads.

Vidhayak Sansad project heads and Shramjeevi Sanghatna block secretaries meet once a month for coordination committee meetings. This committee also plans, implements, monitors and evaluates joint programmes.

Scope of Work

Vidhayak Sansad works in approximately 500 villages in seven blocks in Thane district, two in Nasik district, one in New Bombay, and in some areas of Mumbai. The number of people worked with is approximately 400,000.

The organization has 16 leadership staff and 119 general staff members.

Capacity- and Institution-building Activities

Training of different levels of local leaders, including

◻ Participatory learning camps—training potential leaders of the Sanghatna
◻ Training women leaders
◻ Training panchayat members
◻ Training village-level health workers
◻ Training barefoot engineers at the village level
◻ Training first cadre workers of Shramjeevi Sanghatna

Significant Institutional Linkages

◻ Samarthan
◻ 'Shikshan Hakka Abhiyan' (campaign for right to education)
◻ National Human Rights Commission
◻ Campaign for Human Rights
◻ National Centre for Advocacy Studies

Sources of Ongoing Financial Support

Government of Maharashtra Tribal Development Department
ActionAid, India
Ford Foundation
Unitarian-Universalist Holdeen India Program
Banyan Tree Foundation
Paul Hamlyn Foundation
United Nations Development Program

Address

Usgaon Dongari
Bhatane
Vasai
Thane District - 401 303
Maharashtra
India

Samarthan

Director: *Vivek Pandit*

(Established in 1997)

Purpose

To advocate for the poor and the marginalized at the state level, especially on issues of natural resources, livelihood and atrocities against them.

Overall Approach and Strategy

- ❑ Conduct campaigns on problems affecting vulnerable sections of the society
- ❑ Disseminate information regarding policy matters and programme implementation to social groups and decision-makers
- ❑ Demystify the policy-making process so that people's organizations can participate in it
- ❑ Provide a channel to voluntary organizations and action groups to raise their issues on a wider level

Major Programmes

Samarthan gives priority to advocacy on policy issues concerning mainly the rural poor, addressing issues of Dalits, tribals, women, unorganized labourers, and other vulnerable groups. It takes up campaigns which affect the larger community, interfacing with campaigns for right to information, universalization of primary education and establishment of a state-level human rights commission.

Type of Organization

Public trust.

Governance and Decision-making

The executive committee is the apex policy- and decision-making body, comprising 15 members, with expertise in legislation, the judiciary, media, and other fields. A standing (sub)committee of six members, including the director responsible for day-to-day functioning, determines programme and administrative matters.

Scope of Work

As an advocacy organization dealing with multiple issues such as those involving legislature, bureaucracy and the media, its geographic focus and the number of people it has worked with in Maharashtra are difficult to specify. Staff of 13.

Capacity- and Institution-building Activities

The newness of the organization and staff turnover require the introduction of staff development and training programmes to build the institution.

Significant Institutional Linkages

Vidhayak Sansad
Shramjeevi Sanghatna
Commission on Human Rights (India)

Lok Panchayat
Good access to legislators, bureaucrats and media personnel

Sources of Ongoing Financial Support

Dorabji Tata Trust
Ford Foundation
ActionAid
Unitarian-Universalist Holdeen India Program

Address

87/3, Mumbadevi Municipal School Building
Kalbadevi Road
Mumbai - 400 002
Maharashtra
India

3

Vidhayak Sansad's
Centre for Budget Studies

Director: *Vidyullata Pandit*

(Established in 1997)

Purpose

To provide impartial government budget information to opinion makers, government administrators, legislators, the media and the general public, and to generate a demand for pro-public and welfare-oriented budgets.

Overall Approach and Strategy

The thrust of the Centre is on highlighting trends in state government allocations and expenditures for marginalized sections of the society—notably, tribals, scheduled castes, women and children—especially in social welfare sectors such as primary education, public health, water supply and rural development.

Major Programmes

- ◻ Study and analysis of state budget
- ◻ Presentation of budget analyses to people's representatives at the state legislative assembly, including to leaders of the opposition party and to members of the legislative council

Type of Organization

Public trust.

Governance and Decision-making

Major decisions about programmes and finances are made by the executive committee, with routine functioning overseen by the coordinator in consultation with the secretary and trustee of Vidhayak Sansad. Vidhayak Sansad project heads and Shramjeevi Sanghatna block secretaries meet once a month for coordination committee meetings, to plan, implement, monitor and evaluate joint programmes.

Scope of Work

In 2000, the Centre analysed government social sector budgeting for 13 administrative departments for discussions in the legislative assembly, as well as responding to information requests from social organizations, local activists, and reporters. Staff of 10.

Significant Institutional Linkages

Vidhayak Sansad
Shramjeevi Sanghatna
Samarthan
Campaign for Right to Education

Sources of Ongoing Financial Support

Ford Foundation
Unitarian-Universalist Holdeen India Program

Address

86/3 Mumbadevi Municipal School
Kalbadevi Road
Mumbai - 400 002
Maharashtra
India

4

Navsarjan Trust

Director: Martin Macwan

(Established in 1989)

Purpose

To eliminate discrimination based on caste, assure equality of status and opportunities and ensure the rule of law, not of caste.

Overall Approach and Strategy

- ❑ Community-based, struggle-oriented and constitutional
- ❑ Organizing, mass mobilization, community education, legal redress, external and internal changes, internationalization and linkages

Major Programmes

Training and mobilization of people to demand their rightful share as enshrined in the constitution, addressing individual as well as community issues such as those pertaining to violation of rights, atrocities on women and Dalits, non-implementation of Minimum Wages Act, abolition of manual scavenging and rehabilitation of scavengers, issues of land alienation.

Type of Organization

Public charitable trust.

Governance and Decision-making

A board of trustees is responsible for overall policy. A core committee of senior experienced staff members plays a decisive role in finalizing the overall activities, in a consultative process with Navsarjan's director. Staff members at every level, who are in direct touch with the grassroots communities, are also involved in decision-making.

Scope of Work

Focused on 2,242 rural villages in 11 districts in the state of Gujarat, embracing a Dalit population of 350,000 and 35,000 non-Dalits. The total number of staff is 171—all Dalits, approximately one-third (and increasing) being women.

Capacity- and Institution-building Activities

- ☐ Training programmes for workers on a planned and sustained basis
- ☐ Exposure opportunities for workers to visit other states
- ☐ Periodic evaluation of staff (within the organization as well as external) and of activities conducted
- ☐ Opportunities of cadre training for field staff through decentralization

Significant Institutional Linkages

Centre for Social Justice/Janvikas
Various Dalit organizations through the National Campaign on Dalit Human Rights
International organizations such as Robert F. Kennedy Memorial Center for Human Rights and Human Rights Watch

Parivartan, an offshoot of Navsarjan, which focuses on women's issues

Sources of Ongoing Financial Support

Misereor
Unitarian-Universalist Holdeen India Program
Hivos (Netherlands)
Indo-German Social Services Society
Ford Foundation
Swiss Agency for Development Cooperation

Address

2, Ruchit Apartments
Behind Dharnidhar Derasar, opposite Suraj party plot
Vasna
Ahmedabad - 380 007
Gujarat
India

5

Self-Employed
Women's Association
Mahila SEWA Trust

Founder: *Ela Bhatt*
Managing Trustee: *Renana Jhabvala*
General Secretary of SEWA Trade Union: *Reema Nanavaty*

(Established in 1972)

Purpose

To achieve full employment and self-reliance for the members of
the Self-Employed Women's Association (SEWA).

Overall Approach and Strategy

To organize poor self-employed women in the informal sector
through the dual strategy of struggle and development

Major Programmes

- Organize poor self-employed women through home-based
  workers' campaigns, micro-credit initiatives, and other
  programmes

- ◻ Conduct advocacy campaigns for improved government policies at regional and national levels
- ◻ Provide supportive services such as healthcare, childcare and shelter

Type of Organization

Mahila SEWA Trust is a public charitable trust; SEWA is a trade union.

Governance and Decision-making

Governance and decision-making are the responsibility of the executive committee and the core team.

Scope of Work

- ◻ SEWA operates in 900 villages in 11 districts in Gujarat and in Uttar Pradesh, Madhya Pradesh, Bihar, Delhi and Kerala
- ◻ The population reached is 205,985 in Gujarat and 318,000 in other states through SEWA Bharat (see separate profile)
- ◻ Staff of 300 (all women); 450 members of spearhead teams

Capacity- and Institution-building Activities

- ◻ Conduct leadership training for SEWA's cadres (and for others) through spearhead teams
- ◻ Conduct education and integration campaigns on organizational ideology and philosophy for its members

Sources of Ongoing Financial Support

Government of India
United Nations agencies—UNDP, UNICEF, UNFPA, ILO, WHO
GTZ (Germany)
Ford Foundation
Government of the Netherlands

Government of Canada (CIDA)
MacArthur Foundation
Unitarian-Universalist Holdeen India Program
Income from SEWA (union) funds
Private individual donations

Address

Sewa Reception Centre, opposite Victoria Garden
Bhadra
Ahmedabad - 380 001
Gujarat
India

6

Gujarat Mahila Housing SEWA Trust

Director: Renana Jhabvala

(Established in 1994)

Purpose

To improve housing and infrastructure conditions and the overall living environment of SEWA members.

Overall Approach and Strategy

- Provide legal advice, technical assistance and information on housing, market and shelter-related income opportunities for poor working women
- Influence housing and infrastructure-related urban and rural development policies and programmes in order to bring their benefits within the reach of poor women, by promoting their own institutions

Major Programmes

- Partnership with urban governance to extend urban infrastructure to the poor, including paved roads, toilets, water

and drainage connections, and street lighting for improved health and productivity
◻ Extending housing finance opportunities by setting up systems and formulating policies and guidelines at the national level
◻ Extending improved housing to the informal sector to ensure strong shelters for women and their families
◻ Promoting income generation, low cost technology and disaster-proof housing

Type of Organization

Registered trust.

Governance and Decision-making

Governance is by a trust board comprising nominees from other SEWA organizations. The executive trustee and the coordinator make decisions in consultation with the trust board, on the basis of grassroots demands.

Scope of Work

Twenty-one staff members cover areas in five districts, including Ahmedabad city and rural and drought-prone areas; the approximate number of households worked with is 3,500; and the number of houses constructed is 1,000.

Capacity- and Institution-building Activities

◻ Training of SEWA members to interface and build partnerships with urban governance authorities and to set up and improve housing finance systems
◻ Network building to share experiences and lessons learned through slum upgrading
◻ Staff training through inputs from resource persons and participation in national and international forums on

micro-finance for infrastructure, housing finance for the informal sector, slum upgrading and poverty alleviation

Significant Institutional Linkages

- ❑ HUDCO, HDFC and NHB (housing finance institutions)
- ❑ Ministry of Urban Development and Poverty Alleviation, Government of Gujarat
- ❑ Water and Sanitation Programme-South Asia (WSP-SA) (sponsored by the World Bank and UNDP)
- ❑ Construction Industry Development Council
- ❑ Ahmedabad Municipal Corporation/Urban Community Development, Ahmedabad Electricity Company and Gujarat Municipal Finance Board
- ❑ SEWA family of institutions

Sources of Ongoing Financial Support

Ratan Tata Trust
US Agency for International Development
WSP-SA
Hivos (Netherlands)
CIDA (Canada)
Unitarian-Universalist Holdeen India Program

Address

404, Sakar Four
Opp. Town Hall
Ashram Road
Ahmedabad - 380 009
Gujarat
India

7

Friends of Women's World Banking (FWWB), India

Chief Executive: Vijayalakshmi Das

(Established in 1992)

Purpose

To assist in the formation and strengthening of people's organizations by bringing them into the mainstream of the economy and thereby participating in the process of nation building.

Overall Approach and Strategy

- Promote poor women's access to loans and other financial services through appropriate and sustainable delivery mechanisms
- Strengthen micro-finance institutions in order to provide financial services to the poor on a sustainable basis
- Promote high performance standards among partner NGOs by providing them technical assistance and counselling
- Support innovations and best practices in micro-finance and micro-enterprises
- Expand and strengthen institutional networks for women active in financial and policy-making activities

- Provide a forum for addressing issues related to women and finance
- Enhance the capacity of Friends of Women's World Banking (FWWB) to retain its niche as an institution builder in the micro-finance sector

Major Programmes

- Build the capacity of grassroots women's groups and NGOs to efficiently provide financial services to poor women.
- Provide revolving loan support, through NGOs, to women for activities that lead to income generation and asset creation.

Type of Organization

Wholesale institution closely working with NGO partners—building their capacity and providing them loan support for lending to poor women.

Governance and Decision-making

FWWB is headed by a team of 13 board members, of whom nine are women. The programme team, along with the women programme managers and the CEO, make organizational decisions.

Scope of Work

- Eighteen staff members, of whom 15 are women, work among approximately 29,000 women, predominantly in rural areas
- FWWB reaches out to nearly 80,000 women through the loan support programme
- Provides training to women leaders in group management—FWWB trained about 500 women in a two-year period
- Provides capacity-building in financial management to nearly 100 NGOs

Capacity- and Institution-building Activities

◻ Promoting self-help groups within the micro-finance sector among NGOs, government agencies and national and international development agencies
◻ Developing institution building services for partner groups
◻ Implementing a comprehensive capacity-building programme for credit initiatives

Sources of Ongoing Financial Support

Nabard and Sidbi (Government of India)
CordAid (European donor)
PATH (US NGO)
Ford Foundation
Unitarian-Universalist Holdeen India Program

Address

G-7, Sakar-I Building, opposite Gandhigram Station
Ashram Road
Ahmedabad - 380 009
Gujarat
India

8

SEWA Bharat

President: Renana Jhabvala

(Established in 1984)

Purpose

To strengthen the 10 existing Self-Employed Women's Associations (SEWAs) in India and build new SEWAs by organizing women workers in different parts of the country and nurturing their full development; the focus is on advocacy and advocacy training, so that self-employed women can represent their issues at national and state levels and help build the SEWA movement.

Overall Approach and Strategy

SEWA Bharat is an active link between the different SEWAs, and helps them enhance the capacities of their staffs and leadership and share and replicate each other's programmes. The individual SEWA groups are engaged in organizing women in the informal sector according to the philosophy and strategy of Gandhian values—the joint strategy of trade unions and cooperatives—and placing economic activity for self-employed women at the core of their approach.

Major Programmes

- ❑ Advocacy at state and national levels, including campaigns for a 'National Policy on Home-Based workers' and on issues relating to water (flood and drought), identity cards for informal sector workers (street vendors, rag pickers), among others.
- ❑ Capacity-building of grassroots leaders through exposure and training programmes
- ❑ Strengthening the existing groups and forming new self-help groups

Type of Organization

Federation of membership-based SEWA organizations.

Governance and Decision-making

All decisions are taken at the semi-annual board meetings. The board comprises one representative from each SEWA—all women.

Scope of Work

- ❑ One full-time and six part-time staff.
- ❑ Apart from the staff, there are 318,000 self-employed women members of the constituent SEWAs in 35 districts in Gujarat, Uttar Pradesh, Madhya Pradesh, Kerala, Bihar and Delhi.

Capacity- and Institution-building Activities

- ❑ Organize exposure visits for SEWA staff, community organizers and grassroots leaders
- ❑ Conduct two major leadership training programmes annually for second-level organizers and grassroots leaders
- ❑ Organize women in the informal sector in new locations with a view to creating new SEWAs

Significant Institutional Linkages

Ministry of Labour, Government of India
HomeNet (international network of organizations supporting home-based workers)
National Alliance of Street Vendors (NASVI)
Friends of Women's World Banking (FWWB)

Sources of Ongoing Financial Support

Ministry of Labour, Government of India
Unitarian-Universalist Holdeen India Program

Address

Sewa Reception Centre, opposite Victoria Garden
Bhadra
Ahmedabad - 380 001
Gujarat
India

9

Andhra Pradesh Vyavasaya Vruthidarula Union (APVVU)

General Secretary: Chennaiah

(Established in 1987; became an independent
federation of trade unions in 1998)

Purpose

To promote and protect social, economic, political and human
rights of agricultural workers, marginal farmers, Dalits and Dalit
women so that they may

- Acquire the skills and knowledge to have access and control
  over resources, especially land
- Negotiate for living wages at local and policy levels
- Release bonded labourers
- Promote gender equity
- Work against the practices of untouchability and caste dis-
  crimination
- Promote democratization of the *panchayat raj* system

Overall Approach and Strategy

❑ Organize its constituents under the Trade Union Act—the only legal provision that allows scope for the deprived to unite against injustice

❑ Provide capacity-building and skills development for leaders and other cadres

❑ Organize women, demand their equal status in and share of the national economy, and educate and motivate them to mobilize government resources as a fundamental right

❑ Organize networking, advocacy, mass campaigns, protest marches and rallies to restore Dalit and labourer rights

❑ Take up struggles against untouchability, violence against women, and other atrocities, and for land appropriation, fair wages and release of bonded labourers

❑ Strengthen the membership base of the union and expand its geographical area throughout the state, to sustain the struggles of oppressed groups

Major Programmes

Andhra Pradesh Vyavasaya Vruthidarula Union (APVVU) has concentrated on strengthening its membership; establishing its base in 10 *mandals* (sub-districts); collecting data on land alienation and illegal assignments to the rich; and struggling for land appropriations throughout the state. The other important activity APVVU is engaged in is educating workers and Dalits of the need for a national-level agricultural workers' policy and legislation to bring about social security, minimum wage and employment guarantees. This involves organizing educational camps, foot marches, wall writings, distribution of posters and pamphlets, postcard campaigns for the respective members of parliament, signature campaigns regarding the Comprehensive Agricultural Labourers Act, and national networking—including mass rallies and national consultations with movements from different parts of the country to chalk out common activities.

APPVU has also conducted a survey on the practice of untouchability throughout the state and has submitted its report to the relevant committee appointed by the state assembly. It has also conducted training programmes, mass protests and rallies and a boycott of the celebration of important national festivals to express support for the rights of the poor.

Type of Organization

Membership-based federation of agricultural workers and small farmers' unions in the state of Andhra Pradesh.

Governance and Decision-making

The highest decision-making authority is the 'general body' which comprises all paid-up member unions (two representatives each, one of whom must be female). The general body meets annually and makes all the major decisions, including ratification of decisions reached by the constituent district- and *mandal*-level unions.

Leadership is determined by democratic elections, with 50 per cent of the posts allocated for women and 65 per cent for Dalits.

Scope of Work

There are 280 full-time workers functioning as general secretaries in the 280 *mandals* in 16 out of a total of 23 districts in the state of Andhra Pradesh. Thirty per cent of these are women and 70 per cent are Dalits.

❑ 272,000 paid members, of which 82 per cent are Dalits, tribals or from backward classes, and more than 50 per cent are women. Total membership is approximately 500,000 members.
❑ Active in approximately 10,000 villages (through the 280 *mandals*).

Capacity- and Institution-building Activities

❑ Conduct action-oriented cadre training at *mandal*, district and state levels.

- ☐ Hold regular monthly orientation meetings and action plan reviews.
- ☐ Expose leaders to other mass movement struggles to broaden their understanding of the issues and to foster collaboration.
- ☐ Initiate struggles for land appropriation, release of bonded labourers and implementation of the Minimum Wages Act, Campaign for Agricultural Workers Act, Employment Guarantee Act and the national minimum wage policy.

APVVU also works towards ending the practice of untouchability, violence against women, and anti-people policies by the police or the government. Organizing such struggles at *mandal* and state levels inherently serves to build both cadre and institutional capacity.

Sources of Ongoing Financial Support

Membership dues
DAPPU network of Dalit action groups
FNV (Netherlands Trade Union Confederation)
Unitarian-Universalist Holdeen India Program

Address

No. 6, S.B.I. Colony
Chittoor - 517 001
Andhra Pradesh
India

10

Centre for Rural Studies and Development (CRSD)

President: Hilda Grace (Rani) Coelho

(Established in 1991)

Purpose

To create enabling conditions for the empowerment of the most marginalized people, while strengthening their health, credit and livelihood situations.

Overall Approach and Strategy

- To empower the rural poor, especially Dalits and women, so that they may organize themselves around their issues and struggle for their rights
- To support and develop the human, material and environmental resources of marginalized people

This twin model of organizing and development interventions provides a cohesive perspective and institutionalization rooted in a rights-based approach, with people's participation and local leadership.

Major Programmes

The main thrust of the Centre for Rural Studies and Development (CRSD) is on organizing poor men and women, especially Dalits, at village and *mandal* levels, and linking them to like-minded mass organizations at larger levels. CRSD has organized illiterate rural poor women and men in 111 villages, fostered informal networking at cluster and block levels and assisted registration of a women's union. Organizing men has been more informal and issue-based. The major issues addressed are Dalit issues, drought, right to information and economic (credit) issues, because of the absolute poverty of the populations concerned. A campaign for the effective implementation of the 1989 Prevention of Atrocities Act has been a major activity through the district-level Dalit network initiated by CRSD.

Networking is a key strategy to link mass organizations with voluntary organizations, which in turn increases the collective strength of the oppressed to struggle for their rights. CRSD is involved in two kinds of networking

◻ Networking with voluntary organizations at the district and state levels, to take up issues related to pro-poor policies and to the voluntary organizations themselves
◻ Facilitating networking among people's organizations to protect the interests of the oppressed through education, building linkages and through directly taking up their issues

CRSD has promoted Mandal Mahila Samakya—a membership-based organization in Madakasira *mandal*, which helps women assert their rights and pressure the government to deliver services.

With a thrift and credit programme, hundreds of women are organized into formal groups—they work out the rules by which to run their institutions and begin to feel strength in their collectivity. The loans obtained are mostly for income-generating activities and health care. This programme has prevented many men and women from mortgaging their lands for loans and from dependence on moneylenders. In many villages, the groups have demanded higher wages during the peak agricultural season and have won their struggles. Their asset base has also increased.

Similarly, the health programme trains illiterate women to become strong barefoot doctors and skilled traditional birth attendants. These women provide their services to group members, leading to many women joining the union simply to avail of their services.

Type of Organization

Registered Society.

Governance and Decision-making

The general body of the CRSD Society, the organization's highest entity, elects the seven-member board of directors (three of whom are women, as is the president), decides membership and approves the annual financial statements. CRSD policy direction and programmes are decided through discussions with the concerned staff and community people at various meetings. In general, leadership positions are equally shared, with care taken to promote Dalit leaders and incorporate non-Dalit poor people, in order to increase the membership/support base. People's organizations promoted by CRSD, but not organizationally part thereof, consist of a union and a federation of groups; they make their own day-to-day decisions, while CRSD helps by providing capacity-building and legal advice.

Scope of Work

CRSD works with approximately 43,000 people (more than half of whom are women) in 111 villages in three blocks of Anantapur district, a remote rural drought-prone area of Andhra Pradesh. With only one crop grown per year, there is mass unemployment and migration for more than six months of the year. Twenty-two staff members are involved in the various programmes, of whom six are Dalits and 13 are from 'backward castes'; approximately half the staff members are women. The leaders of the related people's organizations number 241, a significant majority of whom are women and Dalits.

Capacity- and Institution-building Activities

- ❑ Annual orientation and refresher training for all staff on societal analysis, the caste system, gender and on building people's institutions
- ❑ Staff training on laws related to Dalits, women and unions
- ❑ Staff training on individual programmes
- ❑ Training of the leaders of people's organizations on the same and similar issues

Significant Institutional Linkages

Dalita Chaitanya Vedika (a district-level forum working on Dalit issues)
Voluntary Action Network, Anantapur
Voluntary Action Network, India (VANI)
Asmita Resource Centre for Women, Hyderabad
National Women's Organisations Network
National Centre for Advocacy Studies

Sources of Ongoing Financial Support

Unitarian-Universalist Holdeen India Program
Ford Foundation
WaterAid
EZE (Germany)
Asmita Resource Centre for Women

Address

15/212, Court Road
Madakasira
Anantapur District - 515 301
Andhra Pradesh
India

Asmita Resource Centre for Women

Secretary: P. Lalitha Kumari
Advisor: Vasanth Kannabiran
Director of Administration: Dr N. Beena

(Established in 1991)

Purpose

To build a critical mass of politically conscious women and groups to work towards equality.

Overall Approach and Strategy

- ❑ Promoting critical dialogue on current issues, including violence against women (family and public violence, sexual harassment), girls' and women's health and reproductive rights, leadership and political participation, human rights, communalism and globalization; reflection and analysis; advocating on gender issues; providing support to women in need, especially in cases of domestic violence; and critical intervention in movements and struggles from a feminist perspective
- ❑ Working with groups, organizations and individuals by building capacity, training, providing information, raising

awareness and networking, in order to increase collective visibility

Major Programmes

- ◻ Legal aid and counselling for women in distress
- ◻ Training and capacity-building
- ◻ Campaigns and networking
- ◻ Rural and urban outreach activities
- ◻ Research, documentation and publication

Type of Organization

Women's collective registered as a trust.

Governance and Decision-making

A general body, which is responsible for policy-making, oversees the executive body, which, in turn, oversees the core management team. The core management team, along with programme staff, makes decisions concerning overall approaches and individual programmes.

Scope of Work

The team comprises three core management team members and 17 staff, all women and primarily middle and upper caste Hindus, except for one Muslim. Asmita does not have a direct constituency as a support group, but works with groups in almost all districts of Telangana, Rayalaseema and the coastal regions of Andhra Pradesh—around 14 districts in all.

Population worked with includes rural women, Dalits, minorities, women writers, adolescent girls and students, urban poor, the middle class, intellectuals, academics and media staff. The approximate numbers for these groups are—12,000 rural women, 500 urban poor, 150 women writers, 200 minority women and girls, 20 students and 30 adolescent girls.

Significant Institutional Linkages

UNESCAP
National Alliance of Women
Asia South Pacific Bureau of Adult Education
Indian Association for Women's Studies
Indian National Social Action Forum (INSAF)
National Centre for Advocacy Studies (NCAS)

Sources of Ongoing Financial Support

Hivos (Netherlands)
Norad (Norway)
Prince Claus (Women and Censorship Project)
Unitarian-Universalist Holdeen India Program

Address

10-3-96, Plot 283
Street 6, Teachers' Colony
East Marredpally
Secunderabad - 500 026
Andhra Pradesh
India

12

DISHA (Developing Initiatives for Social and Human Action)

Director: Vimla Kharadi
Managing Trustee: M.D. Mistry

(Established in 1985)

Purpose

To work towards the improvement of economic and social conditions of marginalized classes such as labourers, landless people, tribals, Dalits and women.

Overall Approach and Strategy

DISHA believes that unless the poor are organized, it is difficult to alter power relationships and influence the control and use of economic, natural and statutory resources in their favour. To achieve this objective, DISHA has established different forms of organizations, including village-level and area-level groups, trade unions, issue-based groups, women's groups and cooperatives, and has also formed a budget analysis wing. Although these organizations address various issues at different levels, all of DISHA's activities are interlinked, complementary and strengthen each other.

Major Programmes

- ❑ Organizing women *tendu* leaf pickers of Gujarat and addressing their issues, which include obtaining an increased collection rate for *tendu* leaf, checking their exploitation by traders and the forest development corporation for whom they pluck the leaves, and securing compensation against accidents.
- ❑ Unionizing of forest labourers in Gujarat and taking up their issues, especially in matters such as enforcing the provisions of the Minimum Wages Act, regularizing their employment (otherwise treated as 'casual', even for those who have worked for years) and checking exploitation.
- ❑ Unionizing agricultural labourers and taking up issues of non-payment of wages, harassment by employers, work-related accidents, and other questions around their status as landless people living below the poverty line, such as their right health care.
- ❑ Establishing the land rights of tribals and other people from 'backward communities'—people who have been cultivating forestland for decades and have been facing harassment by forest officials in asserting and enjoying their rights; in addition, addressing issues of atrocities and exploitation by the forest bureaucracy, delays in receiving rights of cultivation, and so on.
- ❑ Organizing poor tribals working as labourers in the mining and processing of marble stone in the Ambaji region of north Gujarat, and taking up their issues of employment, socio-economic development, and other day-to-day problems.
- ❑ Organizing immigrant tribals—those who moved from Panchmahal region to Ahmedabad and other cities and worked as construction labourers—and addressing their issues of wage and working conditions, as well as other difficulties and problems arising from their migrant nature.
- ❑ Advocacy at the state level to push for changes in government policies and laws in favour of poor people
- ❑ Developing leadership in various rural areas of Gujarat through a fellowship programme and, through the fellows, the organizing of agricultural labourers, tribals, Dalits, artisans and women around their issues.

Type of Organization

Mass membership-based organization.

Governance and Decision-making

DISHA is governed by a seven-member board of trustees led by the managing director. A core administrative team, led by DISHA's director and comprising tribals and other backward and general castes, coordinates the various activities and reports to the managing director. Decisions on day-to-day activities, as well as those related to the programmes at grassroots and regional levels, are made by the workers' team at the respective group levels. Decisions with wider/state-level implications are made after consultation with DISHA's core team.

Scope of Work

DISHA has 80,000 members and its main area of work is the 52 most backward blocks in eight districts of Gujarat's eastern hilly belt, a rural and interior area predominantly inhabited by tribals. DISHA's fellowship programme covers other regions of the state, mainly Saurashtra and north and south Gujarat, with some 40 fellows working with various sections of the poor, organizing them, creating leadership and, in some cases, helping them form and register local groups.

The total number of DISHA staff is 96 (63 male and 33 female).

Capacity- and Institution-building Activities

A major focus of the organization is building capacity to understand budget allocations of panchayats, from village to district level, and raising advocacy issues around governance at these levels. DISHA's workers also receive exhaustive training in identifying issues, conducting surveys, organizing and mobilizing people, communication means and techniques, negotiating with decision-makers in the government and the bureaucracy, building cases in favour of labourers, and organizing influential events such as rallies and demonstrations.

Significant Institutional Linkages

Various village-level youth, women's and panchayat groups
People's Budget Information and Analysis Service
National Centre for Advocacy Studies
Disaster Management Institute
Janpath

Sources of Ongoing Financial Support

Ford Foundation
Unitarian-Universalist Holdeen India Program
Terre des Hommes (Germany)
Hivos (Netherlands)
Oxfam-UK

Address

9, Mangaldeep Flats, near Parikshit Bridge
Gandhi Ashram Post
Ahmedabad - 380 027
Gujarat
India

13

CECOEDECON

Secretary: Sharad Joshi

(Established in 1982)

Purpose

To facilitate positive social change through a self-directed empowerment process among its constituencies.

Overall Approach and Strategy

Depending on the preparedness of the individual communities, to engage in participatory development programmes, promotion of effective networking among local organizations and jointly tackling issues related to marginalization, poverty and civil rights, through advocacy efforts in Rajasthan and north India.

Major Programmes

- Natural resource management—water harvesting, dryland farming, soil and water conservation, forestry extension and animal husbandry
- Child development and non-formal primary school education
- Prevention and abolition of child labour

- Health clinics, camps and training programmes
- Micro-credit and enterprise development
- Women's rights, agricultural training and leadership
- Development of community institutions
- Advocacy
- Promotion of two network groups—Development Coordination Network Committee and Public Advocacy Initiatives for Rights and Values in India

Type of Organization

Registered non-profit voluntary organization.

Governance and Decision-making

Board of directors with leadership provided by the executive committee through its secretary, directors and deputy directors.

Scope of Work

Direct grassroots work with tribals, Dalits, small and marginal farmers and landless labourers in Jaipur and Baran districts of Rajasthan, as well as work through network partners in additional districts. Full-time staff of 148.

Capacity- and Institution-building Activities

Training conducted through the organization's Human Resource Development Cell.

Sources of Ongoing Financial Support

Government of India departments
Banyan Tree Foundation
Misereor
Inter-Church Organization for Development Cooperation (Netherlands)

The Aga Khan Foundation
Swedish International Development Association (SIDA)
Save the Children Fund
Community Aid Abroad

Address

Agro-Action Development Centre
Shilki Dungari
Chaksu
Jaipur - 303 902
Rajasthan
India

14

Institute for Initiatives in Education (IFIE)

Director: Dr Hanif Lakdawala

(Established in 1994)

Purpose

To make attempts to secularize the society.

Overall Approach and Strategy

- ❑ To involve a marginalized minority to play a proactive role in the affairs of civil society—to come out of their 'mental ghettoes' and 'knit communities'
- ❑ To advocate that the government adopt policies sensitive to minority concerns
- ❑ To activate Muslim women to identify and initiate groups to address their problems

Major Programmes

- ❑ To provide coaching to students—notably girl students—through educational activities
- ❑ To conduct leadership training camps
- ❑ To hold workshops on human rights and women's rights

Type of Organization

A programme of Sanchetna, a registered trust.

Governance and Decision-making

The director and staff make local decisions; larger decisions are made in consultation with a state-level ad hoc committee of 20 members from 19 districts of Gujarat and/or by the national ad hoc committee of 16 members from eight states of India.

Scope of Work

IFIE works on behalf of deprived Muslims and Dalits, with particular focus in Gujarat (six active groups), Bangalore, Varanasi, Lucknow and Hyderabad. The convenors of the groups in three locations are women. IFIE has a staff of three members working through educated Muslims contributing as volunteers.

Significant Institutional Linkages

Various Muslim groups

Sources of Ongoing Financial Support

Bilance

Address

O-45/46, New York Trade Centre
Near Thaltej Cross Roads
Sarkhej-Gandhinagar Highway
Thaltej
Ahmedabad - 380 054
Gujarat
India

Appendix 2

Participant Groups in
'Lessons Learned' Meeting

Participant Groups in 'Lessons Learned' Meeting

Usgaon, Thane District, Maharashtra
January 2000

Andhra Pradesh Vyavasaya Vruthidarula Union, Chittoor, Andhra Pradesh

Astha, Udaipur, Rajasthan

CECOEDECON (Centre for Community Economics and Development Consultants), Jaipur District, Rajasthan

Centre for Rural Studies and Development, Madakasira, Anantapura District, Andhra Pradesh

Disaster Mitigation Institute/Foundation for Public Interest, Ahmedabad, Gujarat

DISHA (Developing Initiatives for Social and Human Action), Ahmedabad, Gujarat

Elgar Foundation, Chandrapur, Maharashtra

Gujarat Mahila Housing SEWA Trust, Ahmedabad, Gujarat

Institute for Development Education and Learning (IDEAL), Ahmedabad, Gujarat

Institute of Women and Child Development, Nagpur, Maharashtra

Jan Jagriti Kendra, Mahasamind, Madhya Pradesh

National Centre for Advocacy Studies, Pune, Maharashtra

Navsarjan Trust, Ahmedabad, Gujarat

Nirmana, Delhi

Parivartan Trust, Vadodara, Gujarat

People's Watch, Madurai, Tamil Nadu

Prajwala, Chittoor, Andhra Pradesh

Prayas, Chinwara District, Madhya Pradesh

Rural Development Awareness and Development Society, Ranga Reddy District, Andhra Pradesh

Rural Development Centre, Beed District, Maharashtra

Samarthan, Mumbai, Maharashtra

SEWA (Self-Employed Women's Association), Ahmedabad, Gujarat

STEP (Society to Train and Educate People's Participation), Mahabunagar, Andhra Pradesh

Telangana Development Studies, Bowenpalli, Andhra Pradesh

Unitarian-Universalist Holdeen India Program

Vidhayak Sansad, Thane District, Maharashtra

Vidhayak Sansad Centre for Budget Studies, Mumbai, Maharashtra

About the Author

John G. Sommer has been actively engaged in development circles in a variety of capacities. Now an independent consultant, he has previously been Dean of Academic Studies Abroad at the School for International Training/World Learning in Vermont, USA. He has worked at both grassroots and senior policy levels with agencies such as the US Agency for International Development, peace Corps, and Overseas Development Council in Washington, DC, and with The Ford Foundation and International Voluntary Services in South and Southeast Asia, respectively. Mr Sommer has also been a consultant to numerous organizations such as Inter-Action (American Council for Voluntary International Action), the Refugee Policy Group, Oxfam-America, the US Senate Sub-Committee on Refugees, and other NGOs and government departments, and is a board member of several NGOs, including the Unitarian-Universalist Holdeen India Program.

Mr Sommer has previously published *Hope Restored? Humanitarian Aid in Somalia, 1990–1994, Beyond Charity—U.S. Voluntary Aid for a Changing Third World,* and *Viet Nam—The Unheard Voice* (co-authored), in addition to numerous chapters and articles in various books, journals and newspapers.